BIRD
BRAIN

OVER 2,400 QUESTIONS TO
TEST YOUR BIRD KNOWLEDGE

TIM APPLETON
&
CHARLES GALLIMORE

WILLIAM
COLLINS

William Collins
An imprint of HarperCollins*Publishers*
1 London Bridge Street
London SE1 9GF

WilliamCollinsBooks.com

First published in the United Kingdom by William Collins in 2018

24 23 22 21 20 19 18
11 10 9 8 7 6 5 4 3 2 1
Copyright © Leicestershire and Rutland Wildlife 2018

A catalogue record for this book is available from the British Library.
ISBN 978-0-00-831574-0

Designed and typeset by Tom Cabot/ketchup
Printed and bound by CPI Group (UK) Ltd, Croydon CR0 4YY

MIX
Paper from
responsible sources
FSC™ C007454

This book is produced from independently certified FSC™ paper
to ensure responsible forest management.

For more information visit: www.harpercollins.co.uk/green

Table of Contents

Preface
Bird Brain of Britain 2018

The Bird Brain of Britain competition at the Birdfair began in 1992 with the title Mastermind and it roughly followed the BBC's successful programme of the same name. Distinguished ornithologists (Chris Mead, Janet Kear, Nigel Collar and Chris Harbard) volunteered to compete and Bill Oddie was the natural question master. It was a success and has continued ever since. The snappier title Bird Brain of Britain was thought of for 1995 and so it has remained. Leading ornithologists continued to 'volunteer' and Bill Oddie continued to grill them, for all but two of the next eighteen years, when Chris Packham was Inquisitor. In the last few years others filling the Torquemada role have been, besides Bill and Chris, Nick Baker, Mike Dilger and Stephen Moss.

The contestants set the Specialist questions (in theory). They are asked to provide ten questions each for the other three contestants so that there are thirty questions to ask. In practice, some questions are the same, some are unaskable and some are not absolutely correct. I have set the General Knowledge questions for the last eighteen years. I am uncertain who really set the questions in the early years before I was involved, but I was under the impression that Tim Dixon set them. However, as he won the 1993 contest, either somebody else did or ...

The original competition was intended to be educational fun, but birders' inherent competitiveness got in the way and it is now a cut-throat battle, the more so since a pecuniary prize of £2,000 was provided by the Catalan Tourist Board in 2007 and subsequently by Vanguard and Swarovski Optik. This is divided into £1,000 for the winner's organization, £500 for second and £250 each for third and fourth. For the first ten years the contestants represented conservation organizations, namely the RSPB, BTO, DOU, BirdLife International, WWT and the Wildlife Trusts. Then other organizations were invited to put forward a hapless volunteer. The four regional bird clubs, ornithological journals, travel companies and optics companies provided cannon-fodder until 2007. Since 2007 contestants have represented the four regional bird clubs – African Bird Club (ABC), Neotropical Bird Club (NBC), Oriental Bird Club (OBC) and Ornithological Society of the Middle East (OSME), with BTO replacing NBC since 2012.

In 2004 we produced a book of the first twelve years and it was suggested another book covering the next fourteen years was fitting for the thirtieth Birdfair. Ornithology has changed quite a lot in the intervening years, with much greater knowledge about birds being acquired, much of it through the use of modern technology. This technology has resulted in frequent revisions of taxonomic classification, much of it confusing to more senior birders, and probably younger ones too. The *Handbook of Birds of the World* and *BirdLife International Checklist* seems to me the most rational taxonomy to follow, and is certainly the most user friendly, and so this has been adopted in this book. As a consequence there are quite a number of revised answers, as the original answers, though right at the time, may now be wrong, or at least different. This has been indicated to avoid confusion (with luck). *Grey italic* is used in the answers section (and a few in the questions too), to indicate the additions and changes.

The IUCN (International Union for Conservation of Nature) Red List categories of threatened birds are frequently mentioned and I have used the recognised abbreviations for the different categories, namely EX, for Extinct; EW, for Extinct in the Wild; CR, for Critically Endangered; CR (PE), for Critically Endangered Possibly Extinct; CR (PEW), for Critically Endangered Possibly Extinct in the Wild; EN, for Endangered; VU, for Vulnerable; NT, for Near Threatened; LC, for Least Concern; and DD for Data Deficient. The term Globally Threatened refers to the CR, EN and VU categories.

31st March 2018 was my cut-off date for updating. In the quiz some leeway has been given to the contestants for date and numerical answers, usually about 10 per cent, but this has been omitted in this book.

I have endeavoured to check and correct and update as many of the questions and answers as possible, particularly with taxonomic changes and matters of fact, particularly regarding a bird's status. However, some answers I cannot verify and others I will have got wrong, and, of course, there will be some with which you do not agree. I accept full responsibility for all these errors of omission and commission. I have sometimes added a comment or an extra gobbet of information which I think is interesting or encouraging or depressing, but I have tried to keep my views to a minimum.

History of Birdfair

The concept of Birdfair was hatched in a local pub in Hambleton close to the shores of Rutland Water way back in 1987. Little did we realise all those years ago that this would start a trend of Birdfair's across the globe.

The aim of Birdfair was to provide a market place for the growing 'industry' of birdwatching, be a meeting place for wildlife enthusiasts and to support a conservation project. Thirty years on Birdfair is the world's largest wildlife event, bringing together over 70 countries and hosting almost 25,000 visitors annually. Birdfair has supported and funded global conservation projects from as far afield as Vietnam to Cuba, Ethiopia to Peru, Myanmar to Argentina. To date almost five million pounds has been donated to BirdLife projects in these areas – an incredible achievement for a three-day event!

On the commercial side Birdfair provides a platform for launching new products from optics, to bestselling natural history books to exotic wildlife holidays. Perhaps one of the biggest surprises has been the growth in eco-tourism – Birdfair is recognised as the 'event' to attend if you are contemplating a wildlife experience of a lifetime. Almost 50 per cent of the 395 stands offer individual and group trips. Although still dubbed as The Birdfair, wildlife organisations also attend representing bats, frogs, plants, butterflies, badgers and more.

Birdfair is more than just a hotspot for the commercial side of Birdwatching, thousands of visitors enjoy a weekend of entertainment. From the moment the gates open until way into the evening there are lectures, games, quizzes, talks, films, debates all supported by our wildlife celebrities. The Wild Zone provides younger visitors with the opportunity to engage directly with the fantastic wildlife of Rutland Water Nature Reserve, whether watching Ospreys, cruising on the water, pond dipping, bug hunting or just enjoying our annual wildlife Pantomime!

BirdBrain of Britain now in its 26th year attracts a huge audience, and thanks to generous sponsorship has helped the participating wildlife clubs raise tens of thousands of pounds for conservation projects in their regions.

The local economy is also a winner, as more and more visitors are staying for the whole three days. Hotels, B&Bs, Campsites, school boarding houses, restaurants bulge to capacity bringing huge financial benefits.

Over the years Birdfair has evolved bringing new attractions such as the highly successful Birdfair Auction raising well over £200,000, the Authors forum and the local produce tent. However none of this would have been achieved without the dedication of our staff and an incredible team of 470 volunteers.

From dawn to dusk for weeks before, during the event and for days after the crowds have left, this wonderful group can be justifiably proud that over the past 30 years they have played their part in creating and running the World's largest Wildlife Event.

30 Years of Global Impact

Every year for the past three decades, the proceeds from Birdfair have gone to a conservation project, selected and managed by the conservation charity BirdLife International. Through your support, these projects have helped to secure a future for some of the world's most threatened bird species and habitats – here are the highlights ...

Year: 1989
Project name: ICBP Stop the Massacre Campaign
Birds that benefit: Migratory birds in the Mediterranean, focusing on the European Robin *Erithacus rubecula*
Amount raised: £3,000
ICBP (rebranded BirdLife in 1993) aimed to tackle hunting and trapping with the first Birdfair project. Birdfair supported an education programme lead by BirdLife Malta, which generated a huge amount of publicity and media coverage in Malta. However, the battle to end illegal bird killing is ongoing.

Year: 1990
Project name: Helping Save Spain's Doñana National Park
Birds that benefit: Eurasian Spoonbill *Platalea leucorodia*, Black-winged Stilt *Himantopus himantopus*, Greater Flamingo *Phoenicopterus roseus*
Amount raised: £10,000
Already beleaguered by agriculture and tourism, Doñana wetlands faced its biggest threat with the proposal of a huge tourist development: 'Costa Doñana'. Birdfair funded a concerted campaign led by SEO/BirdLife (BirdLife in Spain) which successfully halted the development, and financed a visitor centre to promote ecotourism.

Year: 1991
Project name: Danube Delta
Birds that benefit: Dalmatian Pelican *Pelecanus crispus* (NT), White-headed Duck *Oxyura leucocepala* (EN), Pygmy Cormorant *Microcarbo pygmaeus*
Amount raised: £20,000
The Danube Delta's incredible wetlands suddenly escaped the threat of drainage when the new administration declared it a World Heritage Site and a Ramsar Site. However, new wardens lacked basic

equipment. Birdfair funded the provision of binoculars, boat engines, bird hides and other essential kit.

Year: 1992
Project name: ICBP Spanish Steppes Appeal
Birds that benefit: Great Bustard *Otis tarda* (VU), Little Bustard *Tetrax tetrax* (NT), Dupont's Lark *Chersophilus duponti* (NT)
Amount raised: £30,000

Despite supporting three-quarters of the world's Little Bustards, Spain's sweeping grasslands faced destruction by large-scale irrigation schemes funded by the EU. The Spanish Steppes campaign was one of the first truly effective examples of European-level collaborative conservation across the newly remodelled BirdLife International partnership.

Year: 1993
Project name: BirdLife International Polish Wetlands
Birds that benefit: Aquatic Warbler *Acrocephalus paludicola* (VU), Corncrake *Crex crex*
Amount raised: £40,000

Birdfair funded the Polish Society for the Protection of Birds (OTOP, BirdLife partner) to update its directory of wetland IBAs (Important Bird and Biodiversity Area) and seek effective protection for these areas. Funds also went towards Poland's

first reserve in the Swina Estuary to protect Aquatic Warblers. Such efforts have slowed this species' decline in central Europe.

Year: 1994
Project name: Project Halmahera
Birds that benefit: Standardwing Bird-of-paradise *Semioptera wallacii*
Amount raised: £41,000

In 1994, Halmahera was the largest Indonesian island not to possess any National Parks or other protected areas. Focusing on this little-known tropical paradise raised much-needed awareness. Birdfair funded research to pinpoint priority areas for protection. Sadly, civil unrest in the area disrupted the process, but BirdLife clung on, and the first National Park was declared in 2004.

Year: 1995
Project name: Moroccan Wetlands Project
Birds that benefit: Slender-billed Curlew *Numenius tenuirostris* (CR), Marbled Teal *Marmaronetta angustirostris* (VU), Audouin's Gull *Larus audouinii* (NT)
Amount raised: £45,000

Sandwiched between sea and desert, the wetlands along the Moroccan coast are a lifeline for migrating waterbirds. But they are also under pressure from human use. Birdfair funded the better management of key sites along this route, including school and community engagement programmes.

Year: 1996
Project name: Ke Go Forest Project
Birds that benefit: Edwards's Pheasant *Lophura edwardsi* (CR), Crested Argus *Rheinardia ocellata* (NT), Red-collared Woodpecker *Picus rabieri* (NT)
Amount raised: £50,000
Ke Go is the last remaining block of lowland forest in central Vietnam. In 1996, with the publicity and financial backing of Birdfair, the site was declared a nature reserve. BirdLife continues to work in this area to combat the ever-present threat of illegal logging.

Year: 1997
Project name: Mindo Important Bird Area Project
Birds that benefit: Black-breasted Puffleg *Eriocnemis nigrivestis* (CR), Andean Cock-of-the-rock *Rupicola peruvianus*
Amount raised: £60,000
In 1997, with the help of Birdfair, Ecuador's incredibly species-rich Mindo cloud-forest was declared the first IBA in the whole of South America, launching BirdLife's IBA programme in that continent. BirdLife worked with the local community, developing ecotourism

as an alternative livelihood to destructive agriculture.

Year: 1998
Project name: BirdLife International Threatened Birds Programme
Birds that benefit: Blue-throated Macaw *Ara glaucogularis* (CR), Spoon-billed Sandpiper *Calidris pygmaea* (CR), Whooping Crane *Grus americana* (EN)
Amount raised: £120,000
With one in eight bird species threatened with extinction, Birdfair funded research to gather up-to-date information on their populations, creating the landmark book *Threatened Birds of the World*. This sparked public and political awareness and established BirdLife as the avian authority for the IUCN Red List.

Year: 1999
Project name: Rescuing Brazil's Atlantic Forests
Birds that benefit: Seven-coloured Tanager *Tangara fastuosa* (VU), Alagoas Antwren *Myrmotherula snowi* (CR), Bahia Tyrannulet *Phylloscartes beckeri* (EN)
Amount raised: £130,000
43 of Brazil's 103 threatened bird species depend on its dwindling Atlantic forests. The 1999 Birdfair project aimed to preserve them.

Successes included Murici Forest being declared an Ecological Station. BirdLife's activity in this country eventually led to the formation of the NGO SAVE Brazil, now a BirdLife partner.

Year: 2000
Project name: Save the Albatross Campaign – Keeping the World's Seabirds off the Hook
Birds that benefit: Seabirds including the Wandering Albatross *Diomeda exulans* (VU)
Amount raised: £122,000
Albatrosses are the most threatened group of seabird, and one of the biggest threats is death on the baited hooks of long-line fisheries. Birdfair funded the launch of the Global Seabird Programme, which paved the way for BirdLife's highly successful Albatross Task Force.

Year: 2001
Project name: Eastern Cuba – Saving a Unique Caribbean Wilderness
Birds that benefit: Ivory-billed Woodpecker *Campephilus principalis* (CR – possibly still present in Cuba), Bee Hummingbird *Mellisuga helenae* (NT)
Amount raised: £135,000
Cuba hosts 350 bird species, including the world's smallest bird, the Bee Hummingbird (weighing only 2 grams). Birdfair funded vital

research, providing field equipment and setting up Cuba's IBA network, which went on to attract conservation funding for the whole Caribbean.

Year: 2002
Project name: Saving the Last Lowland Rainforests in Sumatra
Birds that benefit: Red-naped Trogon *Harpactes kasumba* (NT)
Amount raised: £147,000
Birdfair funded the then newly formed BirdLife partner Burung Indonesia to identify priority areas of Sumatra's dwindling lowland rainforest for protection. After intense lobbying, the government issued the very first forest restoration licence to preserve one such forest from logging and monoculture. This paved the way for BirdLife's Harapan ('hope') Rainforest Project.

Year: 2003
Project name: Saving Madagascar's Fragile Wetlands
Birds that benefit: Madagascar Fish-eagle *Haliaeetus vociferoides* (CR), Sakalava Rail *Zapornia olivieri* (EN), Madagascar Heron *Ardea humbloti* (EN)
Amount raised: £157,000
The plight of Madagascar's forests is well publicised, but its wetlands are also of huge conservation importance. This project engaged

local people who use the wetlands, working with governments, communities and businesses to draw up legal agreements. These have now expanded into two Protected Areas.

Year: 2004
Project name: Saving Northern Peru's Dry Forests
Birds that benefit: White-winged Guan *Penelope albipennis* (CR), Marvelous Spatuletail *Loddigesia mirabilis* (EN), Long-whiskered Owlet *Xenoglaux loweryi* (EN)
Sandwiched between the Andes, the Sechura Desert and the Pacific Ocean, this isolated, enigmatic region is one of the top ten most biologically unique areas of the planet. Sadly, only 5% of its original range survives. Birdfair funded several successful, locally targeted community-based conservation projects.

Year: 2005
Project name: Saving Gurney's Pittas and their Forest Home
Birds that benefit: Gurney's Pitta *Pitta gurneyi* (EN)
Amount raised: £200,000
For much of the last century, Gurney's Pitta was thought to be lost. The discovery of a population several hundred strong in Myanmar's lowland forests was a fantastic event – but also an urgent one, with the forest threatened by clearance for oil palm plantations. Despite political

unrest in the area, Birdfair-funded fieldwork greatly advanced our understanding of this bird.

Year: 2006
Project name: Saving the Pacific's Parrots
Birds that benefit: New Caledonian Lorikeet *Charmosyna diadema* (CR), Rimatara Lorikeet *Vini kuhlii* (EN), Ouvea Parakeet *Eunymphicus uvaeensis* (EN)
Amount raised: £215,000
Islandbirds are at greater risk from extinction, especially from invasive species. Birdfair funded conservation across the Pacific region, focusing on six threatened parrot species. A major success involved Rima Lorikeets being reintroduced to their original home island of Aitu, where they now thrive.

Year: 2007
Project name: BirdLife International Preventing Extinctions Programme (PEP)
Birds that benefit: Bengal Florican *Houbaropsis bengalensis* (CR), Djibouti Francolin *Pternistis ochropectus* (CR), Belding's Yellowthroat *Geothlypis beldingi* (now VU)
Amount raised: £226,000
Birdfair helped to kick-start BirdLife's ambitious initiative to prevent Critically Endangered birds from slipping away. A highly effective

network linked Species Champions (companies, organisations or individuals providing vital funds to save a species) with Species Guardians (leading targeted action on the ground).

Year: 2008

Project name: BirdLife International Preventing Extinctions Programme

Birds that benefit: Araripe Manakin *Antilophia bokermanni* (CR), Sociable Lapwing *Vanellus gregarious* (CR), Azores Bullfinch *Pyrrhula murina* (now VU)

Amount raised: £265,000

Building on the previous year's success, a further six Critically Endangered birds were highlighted, and the search for Species Champions to 'adopt' them proved very successful. *Birdwatch* magazine devoted itself to the Azores Bullfinch, and Sir David Attenborough himself took on the Araripe Manakin.

Year: 2009

Project name: BirdLife International PEP: 'Lost and Found'

Birds that benefit: Fiji Petrel *Pseudobulweria macgillivrayi* (CR), Makira Moorhen *Pareudiastes silvestris* (CR)

Amount raised: £263,000

Birdfair funded the PEP to establish whether 15 'lost' species survived in the wild – thus informing conservation decisions. A successful example was the search for the Fiji Petrel, which uncovered 8 individuals. The PEP programme has gone on to appoint 46 Species Guardians, protecting 59 Critically Endangered birds.

Year: 2010

Project name: Southern Ethiopian Endemics

Birds that benefit: Liben Lark *Heteromirafra archeri* (CR), Ethiopian Bushcrow *Zavattariornis stresemanni* (EN), White-tailed Swallow *Hirundo megaensis* (VU)

Amount raised: £243,000

Ethiopia's endemic birds are increasingly threatened. Birdfair funded the Ethiopian Wildlife and Natural History Society (BirdLife partner) to work with locals to preserve the Liben Lark's tiny grassland range. Furthermore, Yavello Protected Area was upgraded to National Park status, aiding the White-tailed Swallow and Ethiopian Bushcrow.

Year: 2011

Project name: BirdLife International Flyways Programme – African–Eurasian Flyway

Birds that benefit: Eurasian Cuckoo *Cuculus canorus*, Common Nightingale *Luscinia megarhynchos*, European Turtle-dove *Streptopelia turtur* (Now VU)

Amount raised: £227,000

In the first year of Birdfair support for BirdLife's Flyways Programme, the project focused on well-known birds breeding in Europe but overwintering in sub-Saharan Africa. Birdfair helped the Ghana Wildlife Society to raise awareness, and a new flyway action plan was spearheaded by the Ghanaian government.

Year: 2012

Project name: BirdLife International Flyways Programme – East Asia–Australasian Flyway

Birds that benefit: Spoon-billed Sandpiper *Calidris pygmaea* (CR), Spotted Greenshank *Tringa guttifer* (EN), Black-faced Spoonbill *Platalea minor* (EN)

Amount raised: £200,000

This year's project empowered partners across East Asia to protect key wetlands, used by 50 million migratory waterbirds but encroached upon by human expansion. The Gulf of Martaban in Myanmar – used by half of all Spoon-billed Sandpipers – was declared a Ramsar site.

Year: 2013

Project name: BirdLife International Flyways Programme – Americas Flyway (Prairies to Pampas)

Birds that benefit: Bobolink *Dolichonyx oryzivorus*, Swainson's Hawk *Buteo swainsoni*, Buff-breasted Sandpiper *Calidris subruficollis* (now NT)

Amount raised: £270,000

Across the Americas' grasslands, traditional ranching is giving way to intensive livestock rearing. Birdfair 2013 focused on supporting partners in South America's Southern Cone, with initiatives such as 'bird-friendly' beef certification, and protecting sites of importance for grassland-dependent birds.

Year: 2014

Project name: Saving the Seas and Oceans

Birds that benefit: Macaroni Penguin *Eudyptes chrysolophus*, Audouin's Gull *Larus audouinii*, Pycroft's petrel *Pteodroma pycrofti*

Amount raised: £280,000

Oceans cover 70 percent of the earth's surface, yet conservation actions for marine areas lag far behind those for other environments. Birdfair funded efforts by BirdLife partners' policy staff looking to increase marine conservation. The project was based in Europe and Africa but also included efforts to protect Antarctica and the High Seas.

Year: 2015

Project name: Protecting Migratory Birds in the Eastern Mediterranean

Birds that benefit: White stork *Ciconia ciconia*, Red Knot *Calidris canutus*, Barn Swallow *Hirundo rustica*

Amount raised: £320,000

Roughly 25 million migratory birds are killed illegally each year as they cross the Mediterranean. In order to combat this problem, BirdLife International worked to reduce the scale and impact of the illegal killing by advocating for the strengthening of protective laws throughout the region.

Year: 2016

Project name: Saving Africa's Important Bird/Biodiversity Areas in Africa

Birds that benefit:
Brown Mesite *Mesitornis unicolor*, Madagascar Blue-pigeon *Alectroenas madagascariensis*, Red-fronted Coua *Coua reynaudii*

Amount raised: £350,000

Forest loss is a severe problem across the African continent, and one that is hugely detrimental to birds, as more than two-thirds of species can be found in forests. In order to protect these crucial habitats, the 2016 Birdfair project focused on Tsitongambarika Forest. The area features many endemic species, which makes it biologically extraordinary, even by Madagascar's lofty standards.

Year: 2017

Project name: Saving Paradise in the Pacific

Birds that benefit: Rapa Fruit-dove *Ptilinopus huttoni*, Newell's Shearwater *Puffinus newelli* Polynesian Storm Petrel *Nesofregetta fuliginosa*

Amount raised: 333,000

On the French Polynesian island of Rapa Iti, invasive non-native species are decimating populations of native birds. Money from Birdfair will help BirdLife to remove invasive species in order to restore the islands to their former glory.

Year: 2018

Project name: A Haven for Argentina's Flamingos

Birds that benefit: Andean Flamingo *Phoenicoparrus andinus*, Chilean Flamingo *Phoenicopterus chilensis*, Puna Flamingo *Phoenicoparrus jamesi*

Amount raised: TBC

This year, we're turning Birdfair pink – to celebrate plans to create what will become Argentina's largest National Park, and a safe haven for over a million waterbirds, including three species of flamingos.

GENERAL
KNOWLEDGE
QUESTIONS

2004 A
Martin Collinson – *British Birds*

Answers: page 246

1. Name a bird named after Francesco Cetti.

2. Name three of the signatory nations that have ratified the Agreement on the Conservation of Albatrosses and Petrels (ACAP) under the Bonn Convention which came into force on 1 Febuary 2004.

3. Why specifically has the House Martin been neutered?

4. In which year did *British Birds* introduce the Monthly Marathon?

5. What size of ring would you use to ring a Goldcrest?

6. What was the population of the Critically Endangered Tumbesian endemic Pale-headed Brush-finch thought to be in 2003?

7. 'Wettergulp' and 'pikgulp' were names used by professional Dutch birdcatchers for two waders that wintered in Holland. What species are they thought to be?

8. What is the general colour of most *Hippolais* warbler eggs?

9. What rank was Jacob the Goose, the mascot of the Coldstream Guards (until the last one was run over in the Mall)?

10. Which of the following does not exist: Rufous-collared Sparrow, Rufous-winged Sparrow, Rufous-chested Sparrow or Rufous-crowned Sparrow?

11. What happened to *British Birds* in January 1999?

12. What eagle is named after the fearsome winged monsters of classical mythology, Aellopus and Ocypete?

13. What disease spread to America from Africa in 1999 and is a significant threat to many species of American bird?

14. Which artist designed the 1980 issue of Great Britain stamps, featuring Kingfisher, Dipper, Moorhen and Yellow Wagtail?

15. In which year was *British Birds* first published?

16. What is the resting heart rate of an Ostrich?

17. What bird may be known as a Bodfforchog in Wales and a Salmon-tailed Gled in Scotland?

18. How many Siberian Cranes wintered in Iran last year?

19. What Vulnerable seabirds were taken from Tristan da Cūnha by a South African zookeeper with Foreign Office approval in the past year?

20. In what country, other than Thailand, has Gurney's Pitta been rediscovered (where it is inevitably threatened with deforestation for oil-palm cultivation)?

2004 B
Peter Wilkinson – *BTO News*

Answers: page 246

1. Name a bird named after George Montagu.

2. Which species of extant albatross was found fossilised on Bermuda having been extinguished 400,000 years ago by a sea-level rise?

3. In which year was *BTO News* first published?

4. According to local Peruvian folk lore, what properties does the dried heart of the Endangered Marvellous Spatuletail possess?

5. Three Sedge Warblers, ringed at Litlington, Sussex, in August 2002, were recovered in Finisterre, France, in August 2003. What was remarkable about that?

6. Which of the following does not exist: Northern Double-collared Sunbird, Southern Double-collared Sunbird, Eastern Double-collared Sunbird or Western Double-collared Sunbird?

7. Why has a cock Ptarmigan had his male pride pricked?

8. What size ring would you use to ring a Tree Sparrow?

9. What was the subtitle carried by *BTO News* until dropped in May 1981?

10. What or who are the 'Screaming Eagles'?

11. Where is a bird's pygostyle?

12. Why were three White Pelicans removed from St James's Park in London in 1982?

13. Which British breeding warbler lays unmarked brick-red eggs?

14. What organism produces the toxin that causes outbreaks of botulism in waterbirds?

15. What was the first bird to be depicted on a stamp of Great Britain on the 1946 'Victory' issue 3d stamp?

16. What is the colour of the bill of a downy Water Rail chick?

17. What is the chief threat to the continued existence of the Blue Swallow in South Africa?

18. What connected Battersea Power Station, Chichester Cathedral, Gloucester City Hospital and Nottingham Trent University ornithologically in 2003?

19. What non-steroidal anti-inflammatory drug is strongly implicated in the catastrophic decline in Indian vultures?

20. When does the shooting season for Snipe begin?

2004 C
Chris Harbard – *Birdwatch*

Answers: page 246

1. Name a bird named after Jean François Emmanuel Baillon.

2. What size ring would you use to ring a Blackbird?

3. How much is the annual UK subscription to *Birdwatch* magazine, to the nearest pound?

4. Which species, which was lost to Ireland in the 17th century, does the Irish Wildlife Trust hope to reintroduce with nestlings from Wales?

5. The chief threats, as listed in *Threatened Birds of the World*, are the same for 13 out of 14 of the Globally Threatened species that occur only in the Tumbesian region. What are the threats?

6. Why are some German Nightingales now breaking the law?

7. What species, previously presumed extinct, was glimpsed and heard by a group of birders on Savai'i in Samoa on 5th October 2003?

8. Who was the Assistant Keeper of Zoology at the British Museum in the early 19th century who destroyed many priceless specimens on bonfires because he deemed them 'unwanted' or 'badly preserved', but who nonetheless has a British seabird named after him?

9. Which of the following does not exist: Laughing Dove, Whistling Dove, Weeping Dove or Mourning Dove?

10. In which year was *Birdwatch* magazine first published?

11. What is the cloacal temperature of the little-known Hooded Gnatcatcher, as recorded in the *Handbook of Birds of the World*, Volume 8?

12. Which muscle is the largest in a bird's body and provides most of the force of the downstroke in flapping flight?

13. In which species of seabird was puffinosis first described?

14. What colour are Great Crested Grebe's eggs when newly laid?

15. What bird is depicted on the 2004 South Korean postage stamp, which also depicts the Tokto Islets, which Japan claims as Japanese territory, thereby leading to political squabbling?

16. Apart from Woodpeckers, what other family has Ivory-billed, Lineated, Striped and Bar-bellied species?

17. In addition to habitat loss and degradation, what other threat is considered to be significant for the Rufous-headed Chachalaca in the Tumbesian region?

18. Which tail feathers are elongated in adult Long-tailed Skuas?

19. Which bird features on the badges of the Wiltshire Girl Guides and the Royal School of Artillery, has a pub in Lavington, Wiltshire, named after it and is being reintroduced onto Salisbury Plain?

20. By how much is the shooting season for Woodcock in Scotland longer than in England and Wales?

2004 D
Dave Nurney – *Bird Watching*

Answers: page 247

1. Name a bird called after Gilbert White.

2. What is thought to have caused the skewing of the Wandering Albatross population on Prince Edward Island in favour of males?

3. In which year was *Bird Watching* magazine first published?

4. In addition to habitat loss and degradation, what particularly threatens the Critically Endangered Tumbesian endemic Pale-headed Brush-finch?

5. What species was thought to have a world population of 67,000 birds until 2.5 million were counted at Eighty Mile Beach in northwest Australia in February 2004?

6. What size ring would you use to ring a Tawny Owl?

7. Which of the following does not exist: Inaccessible Rail, Inexorable Rail, Invisible Rail or Snoring Rail?

8. In the first ever issue of *Bird Watching* magazine, what was the title of the article on twitching written by an extremely well-known TV personality (who doesn't twitch)?

9. Where did the extinct pigeon, the Liverpool Pigeon *Caloenas maculata,* live?

10. How many chambers does the avian heart have?

11. Which Founder of a great Cambridge College first described the Dotterel as '*morinellus*' – a little fool?

12. What do Glossy Ibis, Starling, Redstart and Dunnock eggs all have in common?

13. Who killed the Stymphalian Birds?

14. The medical condition of eating unusual substances such as dry paint, coal, excrement etc. shares a name with a common British bird's Latin name. What is it?

15. What were the six geese doing on the 1977 Great Britain Christmas 7p stamp?

16. What species of wader bred in Wales for the first time in 2003?

17. When was the mysterious never-been-seen-in-the-wild Long-whiskered Owlet discovered?

18. How many nests have been recorded in the BTO's Nest Record Scheme in its first 65 years?

19. What was the BTO's Nest Record Scheme originally called?

20. Which feathers are grossly elongated on the wing of the breeding male Pennant-winged Nightjar?

2005 A
David Fisher – Sunbird

Answers: page 247

1. What colour is the bill of an adult Red-legged Partridge?

2. What is the least numerous breeding English corvid?

3. What is 'the Skylark Index'?

4. If you saw a *Balbuzard pêcheur* in France, what would you be watching?

5. To publicise the plight of which threatened group of birds did John Ridgway sail round the world in 2003/04 in *English Rose VI*?

6. Which European country has the largest breeding population of Stonechats?

7. What unfortunate slogan did the charity Animal Aid use to alert people to their feelings about the National Cage and Aviary Birds Exhibition at Stoneleigh in 2004?

8. The range of the Wood Duck in North America falls completely within the range of which unrelated species (upon which it is dependent for successful breeding)?

9. When was Gurney's Pitta last recorded in Myanmar prior to its rediscovery there in 2003?

10. A Razorbill ringed at Bardsey in 2004 had previously been ringed 32, 42 or 52 years before?

11. 750,000 eggs of which species are harvested annually in a supposedly sustainable manner in the Seychelles?

12. Who wrote *Birds of Burma* published in Rangoon in 1940 (and the UK in 1953)?

13. Which species, ringed in Britain, had the most recoveries away from the site of ringing in 2003?

14. Which of the following does not exist – Musician Wren, Harpist Wren, Flutist Wren or Happy Wren?

15. Which close relative of the Okinawa Rail was discovered on 11th May 2004 on the Babuyan Islands in the Philippines?

16. Into what did Aristotle believe that Redstarts changed in order to account for their absence in winter?

17. How many people attended Madagascar's first Birdfair in 2004, to the nearest 1,000?

18. Are there more birds on the British List described as Yellow, Grey or Golden?

19. In which country is Chaplin's Barbet endemic?

20. Are there more species of *Acrocephalus*, *Sylvia* or *Phylloscopus* on the British List?

2005 B
Tim Melling – Naturetrek

Answers: page 248

1. What colour are the legs of the breeding White-winged Black Tern?

2. Which species was ringed most frequently in Britain in 2003?

3. What was the species upon which Edgar Chance did his pioneering work in Worcestershire in the early part of the 20th century?

4. Following the recent taxonomic revision, of the five Houbara Bustards that have been recorded in Britain, how many have been reidentified as Macqueen's Bustard?

5. Where do Greylag Geese breeding in the Forest of Dean go to moult?

6. If you saw a *Chardonneret* in France, what would you be watching?

7. How many wild birds were recorded as imported into the EU in 2000, to the nearest quarter of a million?

8. What was the Spruce Goose?

9. Which species of storm-petrel, believed to be extinct in the 19th century, was rediscovered in 2003?

10. What is Gurney's Pitta's current IUCN Red List categorization?

11. When were Porro prismatic binoculars invented, within 5 years?

12. What bird's song was described by Bobby Tulloch as 'the sound of fairies being sick'?

13. An individual of which species of albatross wearing a 'geolocator' on its leg was recorded to have circumnavigated the Southern Ocean in 46 days, having travelled a minimum of 22,000 km?

14. Which of the following does not exist – Puna Tinamou, Pampas Tinamou, Chaco Tinamou or Choco Tinamou?

15. Common Quail and Turtle Doves in Vojvodina in Serbia are especially threatened by what or who?

16. From where do the eggs used for the current Great Bustard reintroduction programme on Salisbury Plain come (omitting the obvious answer)?

17. Which site won the BTO/Hanson Business Bird Challenge 'Major Wetland' category with 188 species recorded in 2004 – beating Rutland Water by three?

18. What percentage of bird species have been recorded hybridising with other species?

19. What percentage of male Mute Swans are estimated to be killed by other swans in territorial disputes in the UK?

20. What was the occupation of John Henry Gurney, after whom the Pitta is named?

2005 C
Nigel Jones – Ornitholidays

Answers: page 248

1. What colour is the tail of the Azure-winged Magpie?

2. When were Gannets first recorded breeding on Sule Skerry in the Orkneys?

3. Which Western Palaearctic raptor was made 'Person of the week' on the ABC TV *World News Tonight* programme, after visiting Martha's Vineyard?

4. What was the last new species seen by the late Phoebe Snetsinger in Madagascar before her death?

5. What feature of some Feral Pigeons appears to reduce their chances of being caught by a stooping Peregrine when compared with those without this feature?

6. If you saw an *Alouette lulu* in France, what would you be watching?

7. What unique group defence mechanism do Fieldfares *Turdus pilaris* use on potential predators?

8. What is the largest bird family on the Sibley/Monroe classification?

9. What development on Dunmaglass Estate in the Highlands is predicted to decimate the Golden Eagle population in the region?

10. What was the Scottish population of Golden Eagles in 2003?

11. Who first described Gurney's Pitta?

12. Where in the British Isles has the Red-winged Laughingthrush (*Garrulax formosus*) regularly bred since 1996, having escaped from captivity?

13. Name three of the eight key species targeted in the Scarce Woodland Bird Survey conducted by the BTO in 2005 and 2006?

14. Which of the following does not exist – Mountain White-eye, Mountain Black-eye, Barrow's Goldeneye or Barrow's Silver-eye?

15. What bird, according to BWP 'may attempt to force prey off mountain ledges including sheep, chamois, steinbok and even man'?

16. In the hard winter of 1962/63, what was the highest recorded number of wrens observed entering a single nest-box in Britain?

17. Which species of goose could Roman Catholics eat on Fridays in the belief that it was a fish?

18. The BBC reported the rediscovery of which species on 28th April 2005 (unfortunately getting its name wrong)?

19. Where was the only area in England in which Hen Harriers bred successfully in 2004?

20. What was the 2003 population of the Galapagos Penguin reckoned to be?

2005 D
Brian Small – Limosa

Answers: page 249

1. What colour are the legs of a breeding Rose-coloured Starling?

2. What bird is on the back of a £10 note with Charles Darwin?

3. Little Auk chicks are usually fed by only one parent at the end of chick-rearing. Which parent?

4. The local extinction of which species in Alderford Common in Norfolk was blamed entirely on one egg-collector, Daniel Lingham, who was prosecuted in March 2005?

5. And what was his sentence?

6. Are there more birds on the British List described as Northern, European or Eurasian?

7. When was the first BTO 'Inquiry into the Status of the Corncrake or Landrail'?

8. If you saw a *Canard colvert* in France, what would you be watching?

9. Who first described the Moustached Warbler, has a gull named after him and had an Uncle Napoleon?

10. When was Gurney's Pitta first described?

11. A pair of which species constructed their nest in Doha, Saudi Arabia, in 1985 of, among other things, a plastic sandal, two pieces of lorry tyre, two left-hand gloves, a pair of gentleman's underpants (size 32-inch waist) and a complete goatskin?

12. Which of the following does not exist – Sad Flycatcher, Melancholy Woodpecker, Sobbing Pigeon or Lacrimose Mountain-tanager?

13. What is the collective noun for a flock of Great Bustards?

14. What does 'Operation Artemis' seek to protect in the UK?

15. What is unusual about the only mainland breeding site of Jackass Penguin (in Namibia)?

16. In 2001 far more Grey Phalaropes were recorded in Britain than in any previous year. How many?

17. And what was the previous highest score?

18. Most motmots have racquet-like tips of the central rectrices, although they are initially fully barbed along the whole shaft. How does this come about?

19. There are two species of Folige-gleaner restricted to the Tumbesian region of Ecuador and Peru, both of which are considered to be Vulnerable. Name one.

20. How many licensed ringers were there in England and Wales in 1958?

2006 A
Adrian Thomas – WildSounds

Answers: page 249

1. What surprising mammalian threat are Tristan Albatross chicks facing on Gough Island?

2. By what name was *Cecropis daurica* previously known?

3. What is the only bird to be included in the witches' broth in Shakespeare's *Macbeth*?

4. Which European country has the largest breeding population of Rock Pipits?

5. Daisy, who died on 30th October 2002, reared 24 ducklings in 12 years in her capacity as the sole breeding female of wild origin of which species?

6. Are there more species of *Charadrius*, *Calidris* or *Tringa* on the British List?

7. Since 2000 what has threatened the Fatuhiva Monarch?

8. What fate befell a House Sparrow that knocked over 23,000 dominoes at a Dutch televised World record domino stacking event in Leeuwarden (4 million dominoes being the target)?

9. With what bird is Saint Dominic usually associated?

10. Sergei Buturlin was the first ornithologist to discover the nest of which species at its main breeding grounds near the Kolyma River in Russia in 1905 (although a nest had been found in Greenland in 1885)?

11. Which of the following birds do not exist: Tinkerbirds, Tailorbirds, Soldierbirds and Pilotbirds?

12. What does 'squacco' mean?

13. Critically Endangered Sociable Lapwing/Plover chicks are being predated by which species which has spread due to the planting of shelter belts in Kazakhstan?

14. After what are Magenta Petrel and Herald Petrel named?

15. The Sulphur-breasted Parakeet *Aratinga pintoi* has only recently been described as a separate species because it was previously thought to be the immature of which species?

16. How many of the following have had wild populations of fewer than ten individuals: Californian Condor, Mauritius Kestrel, Whooping Crane and Chatham Island Black Robin?

17. The Quarrion or Weero is a common Australian bird. By what name is it more usually known?

18. What kind of farming slaughtered 70 Red Kites, 6 Black Kites, 45 Common Buzzards, 15 White-tailed Eagles and 376 bats among other luckless flying creatures in Brandenburg State in Germany up until August 2005?

19. How many of the 572 birds on the British List are described by eponyms (named after people)?

20. Which of the following gulls' plumage is frequently suffused with pink: Slender-billed, Brown-hooded, Andean and Ross's Gull?

2006 B
Colin Bradshaw – Carl Zeiss

Answers: page 249

1. Who wrote *Swifts in a Tower*?

2. What raptor, not known for nesting in trees in Britain, successfully raised a brood of three in a wire hanging-basket in a tree in Shropshire in 2005?

3. Amorous behaviour with what species led observers to believe that the Black-winged Stilt, that stayed at Titchwell for 11 years was a male (Sammy)?

4. The eggs of which species were collected at Cape Crozier in the Antarctic in 1911 by Dr Edward Wilson, Apsley Cherry-Garrard and Birdie Bowers?

5. Who has a gull and a tern named after him?

6. Are there more species of *Anser*, *Anas* or *Aythya* on the British List?

7. What is a cricket-teal in East Anglia?

8. Who wrote: 'The Dodo used to walk around, And take the sun and air. The sun yet warms his native ground – The Dodo is not there.'

9. In which Red List category is the Ultramarine Lorikeet of French Polynesia?

10. How have German ornithologists been using the bug *Dipetalogaster maximus* for ornithological research?

11. Which of the following birds do not exist: Red Bishop, Pope's Lovebird, Abbott's Booby, Chaplin's Barbet?

12. What is a popinjay?

13. The Imperial Pheasant is now known to be a hybrid of which two species?

14. How many pairs of Bald Ibises were found to be breeding in Syria in 2003?

15. What is the chief threat to the Amani Nature Reserve in Tanzania, after which the Amani Sunbird is named?

16. What was the name of the extinct large flightless pigeon that lived on Rodriguez Island in the Mascarenes until the 18th century?

17. How many of the 572 birds on the British List are identified by a single noun without any descriptive adjective (10% either way)?

18. In 2002 the total of occupied Peregrine territories in the UK was 1,092, 1,292 or 1,492?

19. The 31p 1998 commemorative British stamp, featuring Endangered British species, depicted which bird?

20. Which volume number is the 2004 *British Birds*?

2006 C
Chris Galvin – Swarovski

Answers: page 250

1. H7N7 and H5N1 refer to strains of which avian disease?

2. What genus includes Pavonine, Golden-headed, Crested and Resplendent among its constituent species?

3. What has isolated one of the three remaining populations of Great Bustards in Germany from the other two?

4. In which family of birds were 3 species considered Threatened in 1996, 16 in 2000, and 19 out of 21 in 2006?

5. What mythical species was the late ex-parrot in the famous Monty Python sketch said to be?

6. Are there more Crested Ibis in China or Japan?

7. Which New World warbler, described by Alexander Wilson in 1811, made its first recorded visit to the UK at Paisley in May 1977, just a few miles from Wilson's birthplace?

8. What is the scientific name of the Ancient Murrelet?

9. Spell *Synthliboramphus.*

10. What does *Synthliboramphus* mean?

11. What was the probable reason for the extinction of the Rimatara Lorikeet from the Cook Islands?

12. What bird 'sings on the orchard bough/In England –
now!' in Robert Browning's Poem *Home Thoughts, from
Abroad*?

13. The buds of which of the following variety of pear do
Bullfinches largely ignore – Comice, Conference, William?

14. Which of the following birds do not exist: Calfbirds,
Cowbirds, Bullbirds and Muttonbirds?

15. For what species was a light railway constructed on the
island of Torishima to carry the corpses of slaughtered
birds from the breeding slopes to the beach for the feather
trade in the 19th century?

16. 'Clod birds' was the name used for Corn Buntings by the
father of which previous winner of Bird Brain of Britain, as
quoted in *Birds Britannica*?

17. Name three of the five species on the British List named
after Peter Simon Pallas.

18. With what group of birds is W. L. N. (Lance) Tickell
mainly associated?

19. What was the average autumn count of migrating raptors
through Vera Cruz in Mexico between 1995 and 2001, to
the nearest half-million?

20. How many Zino's Petrel chicks were known to have
fledged in 2005?

2006 D
Stephen Moss – Leica

Answers: page 250

1. The Cuckoo, The Kingfisher, The Finch's Arms and The Old Pheasant are or were all pubs in Rutland. Which one is nearest to the Birdfair?

2. On which English island has the eradication of Black and Brown Rats allowed Puffins to nest successfully in 2005 for the first time for 30 years?

3. Which bird organization publishes *The Auk*?

4. How long after the first Taiga Flycatcher was found at Flamborough Head on 26th April 2003 was the second British record found?

5. Why was the apostrophe in Verreauxs' Eagle recently shifted from before the 's' to after it?

6. By what name was *Lophophanes cristatus* more familiarly known?

7. What insect has become a threat to the Uvea Parakeet (since 1996)?

8. Which species nested successfully in Wales for the first time in recorded history in 2004?

9. And from where did the male originate?

10. What do the 'O'u, Nukupu'u, Maui Alauahio, O'ahu 'Alauahio and 'Akohekohe all have in common with regard to their IUCN Red List categorization in 2000 and 2006?

11. Which of the following birds do not exist: Monkbirds, Nunbirds, Friarbirds and Apostlebirds?

12. Chateau Robin and Chateau Guillemot are wines from which famous Bordeaux area?

13. Why were 60% of the trees in a Vulnerable Superb Parrot colony in Victoria, Australia, felled?

14. In New Zealand the North Island Saddleback, Little Spotted Kiwi, Chatham Island Robin and Chatham Petrel were all confined to single small islands in the last few decades. How many still are?

15. Why is the Bananal Antbird so called?

16. Which country or state's inhabitants are nicknamed 'Crow-eaters'?

17. What is the alternative English name for Gurney's Pitta?

18. Name one group of birds that have large olfactory bulbs in their bird-brains?

19. Which is the largest bird named after Charles Darwin?

20. In what way do the two morphs of Snow Petrel differ?

2007 A
Carl Downing – NBC

Answers: page 251

1. How many Critically Endangered species are there?

2. Which species was recorded from the most 10 km squares in the original 1968–72 Atlas survey?

3. What measurement of Peregrine eggs established incontrovertibly the association between organochlorine pesticides and their population crash in the late 1950s and early 1960s?

4. What was the Birdfair project in 2005?

5. What was the name of the Puddle-duck in Beatrix Potter's famous children's book?

6. How many White-tailed Eagle chicks have successfully fledged in Scotland since their reintroduction to Rum in 1975? Is it 50, 100 or 200?

7. What was the subtitle of the magazine *British Birds* for the first 40 years of its existence?

8. Which of the following birds does not exist – Ursula's Sunbird, Johanna's Sunbird, Mrs Moreau's Sunbird, Mrs Gould's Sunbird?

9. Which of the following is the most important threat to the Bali Starling – hotel development, wind farms or the cage bird trade?

10. What sort of bird is a Bokikokiko?

11. Who was the President of the RSPB from 1985 to 1990 who died in January 2007, and was also a TV quizmaster of a quiz of which Bird Brain of Britain is a straight crib, if less well organized?

12. What bird is known as 'brain-fever bird'.

13. What is a bergander (or bargander)?

14. In which country is the world's largest harrier roost?

15. From which of the following diseases have birds been known to suffer – gout, malaria, tuberculosis and influenza?

16. Which of the following are the subjects of reintroduction schemes in the British Isles: White-tailed Eagle, Golden Eagle, Red Kite, Great Auk and Corncrake?

17. What links 1) nesting Great-winged Petrels and Flesh-footed Shearwaters in Western Australia and 2) nesting Grey Petrels and White-chinned Petrels on Antipodes Island?

18. What is the main cause of death among Blue Cranes in South Africa?

19. The future of which European species is threatened by hybridisation with its non-migratory Japanese cousin?

20. What is the greatest known age attained by a Starling from BTO ringing results?

2007 B
Chris Harbard – OSME

Answers: page 251

1. What bird was responsible for the loss of Eric Hosking's left eye?

2. Which bird, last seen on Lake Alaotra in Madagascar in 1991, was rediscovered in northern Madagascar in 2006?

3. Apart from Malta, of course, which other EU country permits the spring shooting of Turtle Doves?

4. What is the greatest known age attained by a Tufted Duck from BTO ringing results?

5. What is the main ingredient of ambelopoulia in Cyprus?

6. Into which English county are Cirl Buntings being reintroduced from Devon?

7. Aquatic Warblers are now known to winter in Senegal. What guided researchers to look for them in Senegal?

8. What sort of bird is a Balicassiao?

9. In which European country do the majority of Eleanora's Falcons breed?

10. Which of the following birds does not exist – Sapphire Quail Dove, Ruby Quail Dove, Emerald Dove, Diamond Dove?

11. How much did the magazine *British Birds* cost per month in 1907 when it was first published?

12. What was the Birdfair project in 2004?

13. Why is the Providence Petrel so called?

14. Which of the following diseases affects birds – Gull's Disease, Swift-Feer Disease, Thrush, Diver's Paralysis?

15. Which of the following is the most important threat to the Grenada Dove – hotel development, wind farms or the cage bird trade?

16. Name one site where Manx Shearwaters nest in England?

17. Macgregor's Bird of Paradise *Macgregoria pulchra* is not a Bird of Paradise (*Paradisaeidae*) on DNA analysis. What is it?

18. What pigment is responsible for the pink in a flamingo's plumage?

19. Where would you find a Priolo?

20. Name one of the two counties which which have contained the largest English rookeries during the last 30 years.

2007 C
Paul French – OBC

Answers: page 252

1. At least 1,500 individuals of which species were recently observed in Syria, although the estimated world population was previously thought to be only about 400?

2. What is the function of the nasal gland, present in all birds but enlarged in most seabirds?

3. Name one of the flagship species for this year's (2007) Birdfair.

4. When did the second pair of Choughs start breeding in Cornwall following their recolonisation of that county?

5. Which European country has the largest breeding population of Mute Swans?

6. What did French missionaries in Guadeloupe call the fat chicks of Black-capped Petrel, so that they could eat them during Lent with a clear conscience?

7. Which of the following diseases affect birds – psittacosis, puffinosis, wry neck and Parrot's disease?

8. What species of hummingbird regularly breeds in Alaska?

9. Which of the following birds does not exist – Baza, Bozo, Besra, Brolga?

10. Which of the following is the most important threat to the Puerto Rican Nightjar – hotel development, wind farms or the cage bird trade?

11. What was the ornithological name of Sir Francis Drake's ship when he set off to circumnavigate the world in 1577, although it was later changed to *The Golden Hind*?

12. What was the Birdfair project in 2003?

13. Which of the following species have bred in the wild in the British Isles this century: Rosy-faced Lovebird, Rose-ringed Parakeet, Blue-crowned Parakeet and Monk Parakeet?

14. The oldest known Whimbrel was found injured, bitten by a Cape Fur-seal on Bird Island, Algoa Bay, in South Africa in 2005. How old was it?

15. A chick of which species hatched on 1st January 2007 in a captive breeding programme in Haryana in India at least one year before its parents were expected to breed?

16. What Critically Endangered petrel, unrecorded with certainty since 1929, was photographed in the Coral Sea off Australia in 2006?

17. Which 7th-century hermit has been described as Britain's first bird conservationist?

18. When do the Pheasant and Partridge shooting seasons end?

19. What sort of bird is a Huet-huet?

20. To what kind of morbidly obese bird was Billy Bunter of Greyfriars School likened?

2007 D
Mark Andrews – ABC

Answers: page 252

1. What is a Sprosser?

2. Which species bred in London for the first time in 1926 on the derelict site of the Wembley Exhibition?

3. Which book won the BB/BTO Best Bird Book of the Year 2006 award?

4. In which country does the adult Syrian population of Bald Ibises winter (as was recently discovered by satellite tracking)?

5. The average male of which rare British breeding bird can mimic at least 76 other bird species – half of them African?

6. What was the Birdfair project in 2002?

7. Where would you hope to find the Obscure Berrypicker?

8. What disease resulted in a permanent ban on the import of wild birds into the EU in January 2007?

9. What Critically Endangered species was rediscovered after 100 years by a shepherd looking for a lost goat in Peru in 1977?

10. Which of the following birds does not exist – Boubou, Brubru, Bobo, Boobook?

11. Which of the following is the most important threat to the Lear's Macaw – hotel development, wind farms or the cage bird trade?

12. Which European warbler spends 23.7 minutes per copulation on average?

13. How old was a Lesser Flamingo found dead at Lake Bogoria in Kenya in July 2003 that had been ringed by Leslie Brown and Alan Root as a chick?

14. Roughly how many eggs, to the nearest 5,000, of the Horseshoe Crab does a Knot require per day to sustain it at its fuelling stop in Delaware Bay on its spring migration?

15. A group of Belgians is campaigning to allow the trapping of which songbird because wild birds sing better in cages than captive-bred birds?

16. In 2004, what species of raptor electrocuted itself on power lines at Santa Clarita, Los Angeles, and fell burning to the ground, starting a fire which burnt 2,300 ha, necessitating the evacuation of 1,600 homes?

17. By what name was *Poecile palustris* formerly known?

18. What is closest relative to the Kagu of New Caledonia on both DNA and morphological evidence?

19. Of Hawaii's 34 species of Honeycreeper, are 3, 13 or 23 now extinct?

20. The WWF (World Wildlife Fund/Worldwide Fund for Nature) was founded in 1961 by Julian Huxley, Max Nicholson and two other ornithologists. Name one.

2008 A
Martin Fowlie – NBC

Answers: page 252

1. Which project is being supported by Birdfair this year?

2. Is Lincoln's Sparrow named after President Abraham Lincoln?

3. Which island in the British Isles has only single records of Goosander, Marsh Tit, Eastern Phoebe and Ancient Murrelet?

4. What Critically Endangered species from Brazil was depicted on last year's Birdfair poster?

5. Which British bird is potentially under threat from Tree Mallow which has spread in the UK due to amelioration of the climate?

6. What sort of flightless ducks have been found to migrate from the Pacific to the Atlantic via the Bering Strait since 1992?

7. For what purpose are seriemas, screamers and trumpeters used by humans in South America?

8. Name one of the three archipelagos that have twelve or more Critically Endangered species.

9. What colour is the iris of the Woodpigeon?

10. Which of the following is not extinct: Hawaiian Rail, Tahiti Rail, British Rail, New Britain Rail?

11. What anti-inflammatory drug is in use in veterinary practice in Tanzania, although it has already decimated the vulture population in India?

12. With what product are the piquero, camanay, alcatraz and guanay associated?

13. Which Critically Endangered species has *in focus* championed, as part of BirdLife International's Guardians and Champions project?

14. What plumage difference distinguishes the male Ptarmigan from the female in winter?

15. Which Critically Endangered parrot has recently bred in the wild following translocation?

16. Roatelo, meaning two-three in Malagasy, is an alternative name for which Madagascan endemic birds after their habit of going around in small groups of two or three?

17. Beside the Mangrove Finch, what is the other Critically Endangered passerine in the Galapagos?

18. Which oystercatchers have a white neck collar?

19. What bird is named after Madame Dumont d'Urville?

20. In what year did Scottish Crossbill become a species on the British List, within three years?

2008 B
David Murdoch – OSME

Answers: page 253

1. Which project was supported by Birdfair last year?

2. What colour is the lower mandible of the female Common Kingfisher?

3. What is a bleeding-heart?

4. What was the ornithological surname of the French winner of the gold medal in the 5,000 metres in the 1920 Olympic Games?

5. In which country was a flock of 3,200 Sociable Lapwings counted in 2007?

6. What ornithological event is believed to have caused the huge increase in the population of White-footed Mouse in the USA, resulting in an increase in Lyme disease, as the mouse is a vector of deer-ticks?

7. What Critically Endangered species from Mexico was depicted on last year's Birdfair poster?

8. Why was the Olive-tree Warbler in Shetland in August 2006 less exciting for the finders than it might have been for a British 'first'?

9. Is the estimated tonnage of lead shot used by hunters round the Mediterranean each year 6,000, 60,000 or 600,000 tonnes?

10. Which of the following is not extinct: Norfolk Starling, Tanimbar Starling, Mysterious Starling, Reunion Starling?

11. Which Critically Endangered species has Swarowski championed as part of BirdLife International's Guardians and Champions project?

12. What is Scotch woodcock?

13. Name one of the three or four Critically Endangered species with a population thought to be greater than 30,000 individuals.

14. What colour is the iris of an Osprey?

15. Is the Stanley Bustard named after the 19th century British Prime Minister, Edward Stanley?

16. What name does the International Ornithological Congress recommend that we now use for Rock Dove / Rock Pigeon /Feral Pigeon/*Columba livia*?

17. Name one country, outside Africa, where Lesser Flamingo has bred in historical times?

18. Who illustrated both T. A. Coward's *Birds of the British Isles and their Eggs* and Miss S. Vere Benson's *Observer's Book of British Birds*?

19. What was the commonest non-natural (human-related) cause of death among Spanish Imperial Eagles between 1989 and 2004?

20. What is the Red Sea Warbler more commonly called?

2008 C
Paul Stancliffe – BTO

Answers: page 253

1. Which project will be supported by Birdfair next year?

2. Where else is an Azure-winged Magpie azure apart from the wings?

3. Which species of bird caused the greatest loss of human life in an air strike when 62 people were killed when birds brought down an Eastern Airlines Lockheed Electra in Boston, Massachusetts, in 1960?

4. Is Wilson's Warbler named after Woodrow Wilson, the former US president?

5. In which country was the world's largest Arctic Tern colony of over 50,000 pairs in 1950, which had been completely exterminated by 2000 due to egg-collecting?

6. Which Old World warbler breeds in the New World?

7. What species of bird has learned to peck around the tail of brooding Nazca Boobies in the Galapagos in order to drink the blood thereby produced?

8. What is urohidrosis?

9. What Critically Endangered species from Africa was depicted on last year's Birdfair poster?

10. Which of the following does not exist: Golden-crowned Emerald, Sapphire-spangled Emerald, Ruby-necklaced Emerald, Coppery-headed Emerald?

11. In 1930 what happened when the last remaining female Laysan Duck had her eggs destroyed by a Bristle-thighed Curlew?

12. Which Critically Endangered species has *Birdwatch* magazine championed as part of BirdLife International's Guardians and Champions project?

13. What was the ornithological-sounding surname of the New Zealand winner of the silver medal in the 5,000 metres in the 1976 Olympic Games?

14. What object attached to a White Stork shot in Mecklenburg in Germany in 1822 gave a clue that storks wintered in Central Africa?

15. What colour is the iris of the Stock Dove?

16. Which country is home to the most species of Critically Endangered hummingbird?

17. Who was Roger Tory Peterson's companion on a 25,000 mile tour of North America in 1953, resulting in the book *Wild America*?

18. What happened to the first captive-bred Philippine Eagle to be released in the Philippines?

19. What name does the International Ornithological Congress (IOC) recommend that we now use for (Common) Crossbill *Loxia curvirostra*?

20. In what year did the Cattle Egret colonise South America? Give the decade.

2008 D
Pete Leonard – ABC

Answers: page 254

1. How many Critically Endangered species are there?

2. The dark markings on the throat of the male Common Quail are usually compared with what nautical object?

3. What bird did American hunters call the 'dough bird', on account of the soft dough-like texture of its fat on its autumn migration, when millions were slaughtered?

4. Is the Bushtit named after the American president?

5. Which race of Peregrine breeds in the British Isles?

6. On 17th August 1768 (240 years ago tomorrow), Gilbert White described three species, previously considered to be one species, in a letter to Thomas Pennant. What were they?

7. In 1941 what American passerines did Vera Lynn predict would be over the White Cliffs of Dover?

8. What Critically Endangered species from Asia was depicted on last year's Birdfair poster?

9. When Konrad von Gesner published a drawing and description of a now Critically Endangered bird in 1555, the general response was that it was a hoax. What was this outlandish bird?

10. In Navarra in north-east Spain, what species was most frequently killed by 271 wind-turbines between 2000 and 2002?

11. Which of the following does not exist: Thrush Nightingale, Nightingale Finch, Nightingale Wren, Nightingale Bunting?

12. What species has most recently been classified as Critically Endangered?

13. Name one of the four genera with the dubious honour of having four Critically Endangered species.

14. Which Critically Endangered species has *Wildsounds* championed as part of BirdLife International's Guardians and Champions project?

15. In which European country does approximately half the world population of Red Kite breed?

16. By what name was *Cyanistes caeruleus* more familiarly known?

17. What colour is the iris of a Common Kestrel?

18. What is a 'faeder' when applied to Ruff?

19. In what year did the Cattle Egret colonise North America (Florida)? Give the decade.

20. What killed 17 of the 18 young Whooping Cranes in the migratory eastern population of Whooping Cranes in Florida in 2007?

2009 A
Jez Bird – OBC

Answers: page 254

1.   What is the principal diet of the Acorn Woodpecker in winter?

2.   What is the principal diet of the Sandwich Tern?

3.   Are there more Critically Endangered birds or Critically Endangered amphibians?

4.   What are 'duck stamps' used for in the USA?

5.   The activities of which species of bird led to the abandonment of a Parliamentary Bill in the House of Commons in 1607?

6.   Which has the longer bill – Sword-billed Hummingbird or Greenshank?

7.   Who, born 100 years ago in September, first described the Greenland White-fronted Goose?

8.   Which former Warden of Dungeness Bird Observatory and subsequent Head of Reserves Management at the RSPB died on 26th March 2009?

9.   What is a haggard hawk or falcon?

10. Which of the following birds does not exist: Sicklebill, Scythebill, Spadebill, Secateurbill?

11. From what protein are feathers made principally?

12. What birds may be Bronze-winged, Comb-crested and Pheasant-tailed?

13. To what was John Clare referring when he wrote: 'Ah, could I see a spinney nigh/A paddock riding in the sky Above the oaks, in easy sail/On stilly wings and forked tail'?

14. What red-legged birds are depicted on the coat of arms of Canterbury?

15. How many species of bunting are included in the suite of 19 birds included in the Farmland Bird Index?

16. For a bonus, name two of the three.

17. Who is Chief Executive of the Royal Society for the Protection of Birds?

18. When was the Ornithological Society of the Middle East founded?

19. Which wader first bred in Britain in 1938 and now numbers a few hundred breeding pairs?

20. What European country has the Great Bustard as its national bird?

2009 B
Martin Fowlie – NBC

Answers: page 255

1. What is the principal diet of the Yellow-bellied Sapsucker (outside the breeding season)?

2. What is the principal diet of the Bananaquit?

3. Who is the Chief Executive Officer of BirdLife International?

4. What birds can be Bronze-winged, Double-banded and Cream-coloured?

5. Who, born 300 years ago, on 10th March, has a jay, an eider and a sea-cow named after him?

6. Which has the longer wing – Corncrake or Common Swift?

7. Do birds have a spleen?

8. Which of the following birds does not exist: Bald Parrot, Bald Bulbul, Bald Eagle, Bald Ibis?

9. What is snarge?

10. Name two Critically Endangered species which occur in continental USA (if not yet extinct)?

11. For a bonus, name two more.

12. How many different Rosses are Ross's Goose, Ross's Gull and Ross's Turaco named after?

13. Which is named after who?

14. What migrated from Beech Grove to The Nunnery in 1991?

15. What is a falconer's hawk doing if it is having a jenk?

16. Apart from the Rook, which other corvid is included in the Farmland Bird Index?

17. Who, born 200 years ago this September, wrote of the Eagle that: 'He clasps the crag with crooked hands;/Close to the sun in lonely lands, Ring'd with the azure world, he stands'?

18. How many years ago was the Oriental Bird Club founded?

19. When did Cetti's Warbler first breed in Britain in recent times, within three years?

20. In which country can you see both Groundscraper Thrush and Cloud-scraping Cisticola?

2009 C
Richard Prior – OSME

Answers: page 255

1. What is the principal diet of the Snail Kite?

2. What is the principal diet of the Morepork?

3. Who, born 200 years ago on 12th February, has a tinamou, a rhea and some finches named after him?

4. By what ornithological name was the French singer Edith Piaf known?

5. How does the Hoatzin differ from other vegetarian birds in the way it breaks up the tough leaves that comprise its diet?

6. Which species bred for the first time in Britain in Somerset in 2008?

7. How many pairs nested?

8. For what group of birds are tori lines used as a conservation measure?

9. Which of the following birds does not exist: Scimitarbill, Spearbill, Shoebill, Sheathbill?

10. In 2008 an electronic tag from a Steelhead Salmon, marked at the Columbia River hatchery in Oregon in 2006, was found by the nest of which species of bird on Mokonui Island in New Zealand, 10,000 kms from Oregon?

11. Which has the longer leg (tarsus) – Black-winged Stilt or

Mute Swan?

12. After 1993 what led to the marked increase in the capture of Endangered Javan Hawk Eagles as status symbols?

13. How many species of finch are included in the Farmland Bird Index?

14. For a bonus, name two of the three.

15. The specific name of the Critically Endangered Alagoas Antwren is named after which eminent ornithologist who died on 4th February 2009?

16. What birds may be Sharp-tailed, White-rumped, Buff-breasted and Spoon-billed?

17. Who is the President of the British Ornithologists' Union?

18. When was the African Bird Club founded?

19. What now Critically Endangered species received protection as early as 1504 from the Archbishop of Salzburg?

20. Which Critically Endangered passerine is confined to a 7 sq km island in the Atlantic?

2009 D
Nigel Redman – ABC

Answers: page 255

1. What is the principal diet of the European Bee-eater?

2. What is the principal diet of the Macaroni Penguin?

3. Which American sparrow is named after Charles Darwin's mentor at Cambridge?

4. How many ossicles do birds have in their middle ear?

5. Which has the longer tail – Caspian Tern or Cuckoo?

6. Name two of the three species of Critically Endangered ducks that are not confined to islands?

7. For a bonus, name the third.

8. What mammal was responsible for the deaths of both Prince Ruspoli and Johan Wahlberg after whom a turaco and eagle are named?

9. Which well-known ornithologist, who died this year, wrote *The Private Life of the Street Pigeon* in 1979 and also recorded *Witherby's Sound Guide to British Birds* with Myles North?

10. Which of the following birds does not exist: Kiwi, Pewee, Weewee, Iiwi?

11. What is a sod in Shetland?

12. What is the connection between the Silver Invicta, the Golden Olive Bumble and the (Eurasian) Jay?

13. What is the matter with a falconer's hawk if it has craye?

14. What birds can be Broad-tailed, Pin-tailed, Shaft-tailed and Straw-tailed?

15. Which philosopher and ornithologist, born 2,393 years ago, is commemorated in the Latin name of a British seabird?

16. Who is the Director of the British Trust for Ornithology?

17. Which is the only warbler included in the Farmland Bird Index?

18. When was the Neotropical Bird Club founded?

19. Which is the only species of crane that has an increasing population trend?

20. Prior to the 2001 record of Magpie on St Martin's, how many had previously been recorded on Scilly?

2010 A
Pete Morris – ABC

Answers: page 255

1. Of which American state is the Rhode Island Red the state bird?

2. In which decade did Sir Peter Scott first notice the significance of bill patterns to enable individual Bewick's Swans to be told apart?

3. When was the Ramsar Convention on Wetlands signed? Was it 1961, 1971 or 1981?

4. In which country is Ramsar after which the International Convention on Wetlands is named?

5. In which county have both Pacific auks on the British List been recorded?

6. Where would you go to see *Troglodytes troglodytes hirtensis*?

7. What material did the Japanese use to make mist-nets for catching birds for food during World War II, and which were subsequently adopted in 1956 for ringing?

8. Which of the following birds does not exist: Minute Piculet, Miniature Tit-babbler, Tiny Hawk, Small Minivet?

9. What species of swan was found dead at Cellardyke from avian flu in 2006?

10. What species was it at first thought to be?

11. What species has hybridised with chickens, guineafowl, two species of goose, 41 species of duck and has also indulged in homosexual necrophilia?

12. Kakapo only breed when the fruit of which trees are superabundant?

13. 'On a tree by a river a little tom-tit – sang "willow, titwillow titwillow …"' comes from *The Mikado* by Gilbert and Sullivan. What was the tom-tit?

14. What is the title of the African Bird Club journal?

15. In 1456 what finch species was the first to be involved in singing competitions in Europe?

16. What birds can be Velvet-mantled, White-bellied, Crow-billed, Fork-tailed or Hair-crested?

17. What is ptilochronology used to measure?

18. Who wrote the foreword for either the first or the second Atlas of Breeding Birds of Britain and Ireland?

19. In which country is BANCA the BirdLife partner?

20. What is a 'mock nightingale' according to Gilbert White?

2010 B
James Eaton – OBC

Answers: page 256

1. Where would you go to see *Troglodytes troglodytes zetlandicus*?

2. Which adult passerine on the British List has red underparts and a broken eye-ring?

3. Of which American state is the Carolina Wren the state bird?

4. Which Finnish biologist had an Endangered Asian wader and the most popular variety of Christmas tree named after him?

5. What was the first British-ringed bird to be recovered abroad?

6. What bird was Shelley referring to when he wrote: 'Hail to thee, blithe spirit!/Bird thou never wert,/That from heaven, or near it/Pourest thy full heart/In profuse strains of unpremeditated art.'

7. Which mammal have Great Tits been found regularly killing and eating in the Bukk Mountains in Hungary?

8. Which of the following birds does not exist: Cherry-throated Tanager, Orange-throated Tanager, Strawberry-spectacled Tanager, Lemon-spectacled Tanager?

9. 183 kites and 285 buzzards were killed between 1807 and 1816 by game-keeping interests at the Burley Estate. Where is the Burley Estate?

10. What was the ornithological discovery of Edward Jenner (who introduced vaccination against smallpox), which resulted in his election to the Royal Society in 1789?

11. What is the ornithological traditional bingo call for 22?

12. Who was the compiler of the first *Atlas of Breeding Birds in Britain and Ireland*?

13. When was the last wild California Condor taken into captivity to join a captive-breeding programme? Was it 1987, 1989 or 1991?

14. In which country was the only certain specimen of the Red Sea Swallow found (in 1984)?

15. What bird was Gilbert White referring to when he wrote about a Jar Bird?

16. What is the journal of Neotropical Bird Club?

17. What is the BirdLife partner in Turkey?

18. To discuss which Critically Endangered species did the Prime Ministers of Japan and China (Shinzo Abe and Wen Jiabao) meet in February 2007?

19. Which English king, born over a thousand years ago, has a wader named after him?

20. What method does the Hooded Pitohui in New Guinea use to deter feather-lice and predators?

2010 C
Stuart Elsom – NBC

Answers: page 256

1. Where would you go to see *Troglodytes troglodytes hebridensis*?

2. Which former British Foreign Secretary has an ornithological institute named after him?

3. What catastrophic event is believed to have caused a steep decline in the population of Nicobar Megapodes on the Nicobar Islands in the last ten years?

4. Who wrote, while sitting in a churchyard: 'Save that from yonder ivy-mantled tower/The moping owl does to the moon complain/Of such as, wandering near her secret bower,/Molest her ancient solitary reign'?

5. How many rings have BTO ringers used in the last century (to the nearest 5 million)?

6. How many tonnes of metal is that?

7. Which former winners of the Bird Brain of Britain have written the foreword to a volume of *Handbook of Birds of the World*?

8. Of which American state is the California Gull the state bird?

9. What is the greatest threat to the Critically Endangered Chinese Crested Tern?

10. What was Lieutenant Cal Rogers's claim to ornithological fame in 1912?

11. In which country is BirdLife's affiliated partner O le Si'osi'omaga Society Incorporated?

12. Which of the following birds does not exist: Painted Tody-Flycatcher, Painted Tanager, Painted Bunting, Painted Stork?

13. What are 'tendelles' used for, quite legally, in France?

14. How many species in the family Rallidae are flightless? Is it 22, 32 or 42?

15. The mother of Zeus gave her name to which South American species?

16. What wader species has flown non-stop from Alaska to New Zealand in 2007, a distance of 11,600 kms (7,200 miles), confirmed by satellite tracking?

17. What is the journal of the Ornithological Society of the Middle East?

18. Which species, whose nest was first described by James Bond, has just been reclassified as Critically Endangered by IUCN?

19. In which European country have both Bateleur and Dunn's Lark been recorded?

20. Which artist designed the 1980 British stamps commemorating the centenary of the Wild Bird Protection Act?

2010 D
Nick Moran – OSME

Answers: page 256

1. Name one of the two women who have been President of the RSPB?

2. What years does the current BTO/SOC/Birdwatch Ireland Atlas cover?

3. What was the first British bird to be fitted with a numbered ring (on 8th May 1909)?

4. Where would you go to see *Troglodytes troglodytes fridariensis*?

5. Which species of pelican bred in Britain during the Bronze Age (say 2000–1000 BCE)?

6. The Long-billed Murrelet in Devon in November 2006 was the second European record for this Pacific species. In which country was the first European record?

7. What Critically Endangered species has hatched a chick on Nonsuch Island for the first time in nearly 400 years following a translocation programme?

8. Which of the anti-inflammatory drugs – Meloxicam and Ketoprofen – is not thought to be toxic to vultures?

9. Which of the following birds does not exist: Obscure Honeyeater, Mysterious Greenbul, Cryptic Antthrush, Elusive Antpitta?

10. Guano stains, visible on Landsat satellite images, have revealed ten new colonies of which penguin species?

11. Where may Apus (Bird of Paradise), Tucana (Toucan) and Pavo (Peacock) all be found together?

12. What bird has been variously known as *Anser magellanicus*, Tossefugl, Isarokitosk and Garefowl?

13. In what way do Catbirds of the genus *Ailuroedus* differ from other Bowerbirds of the family Ptilonorhynchidae?

14. Which is the only character on the Cluedo board named after a bird?

15. What is the BirdLife partner in the Philippines?

16. Who described the Kestrel as '… morning's minion, kingdom of daylight's dauphin, dapple-dawn-drawn Falcon …'?

17. Of which American state is the Roadrunner the state bird?

18. What special threat did the football World Cup pose for Cape Vultures?

19. What birds may be American, New Zealand, Indian, Japanese or European?

20. The feathers of which New Zealandbird are used to make the Maori cloak called a kahu-hihi?

2011 A
Steve Rooke – ABC

Answers: page 257

1. In which UK Overseas Territory is the St Helena Plover to be found?

2. In which UK Overseas Territory is the Vulnerable Cobb's Wren to be found?

3. Which introduced species, which appears on the cover of a respected British ornithological journal, is now regarded as a pest in western France and the Florida Everglades, where eradication is currently proposed?

4. Which group of birds is threatened in India by black-magic practitioners and the obsession of their affluent middle class with *Harry Potter*?

5. In which century did the practice of swan-upping on the River Thames begin? Was it 12th, 14th or 16th century?

6. Name one of the two livery companies that own the Mute Swans on the Thames and partake in the annual swan-upping census.

7. Name the other.

8. What organization did T. Gilbert Pearson found with Jean Delacour in 1922?

9. What was the volume of the egg of the Madagascar Elephant bird *Aepyornis maximus* – 4 pints, 8 pints or 16 pints?

10. What species has been most affected by the wreck of the 75,000 ton soya-bean carrying, Maltese registered, Greek captained, Filipino crewed MS *Oliva* on Nightingale Island, Tristan da Cunha archipelago, on 16th March this year – the latest ship to cause environmental havoc?

11. Which of the following birds do not exist: Kate's Warbler, Adelaide's Warbler, Virginia's Warbler, Grace's Warbler?

12. Name two of the three seabird species more than half of whose world population breed in the British Isles.

13. Name the third.

14. Which bird is called 'Trifingra mevo' in Esperanto?

15. '*Teevo cheevo cheevio chee*:/O where, what can that be? *Weedio-weedio*: there again!/So tiny a trickle of song-strain' was how Gerald Manley Hopkins described which uncommon passerine's song?

16. What are whalebirds?

17. Which was the first species of migrant passerine to be tracked on its migration using a geolocator (weighing 1 g)?

18. What species was discovered in 1973 and almost certainly became extinct in 2004 in Hawaii?

19. Which conservation convention celebrated its 40th anniversary on 2nd February this year?

20. What is the only extant endemic bird species on Aldabra?

2011 B
Chris Balchin – NBC

Answers: page 257

1. In which UK Overseas Territory is the Pitcairn Reed Warbler to be found?

2. In which UK Overseas Territory is the Vulnerable Forest Thrush to be found?

3. The Recommended English Name decreed by the International Ornithological Union for Wood Lark is now Woodlark (one word). Is the Skylark similarly a one word bird?

4. Guy Bradley was, arguably, the first human martyr in the cause of bird conservation when he was murdered in 1905 in Florida while protecting which species?

5. What group of birds were the first to be protected by an Act of Parliament in Britain in 1869?

6. Willock, marrot and coulterneb are three species protected by the Act. To which family do they belong?

7. *Vultur gryphus* is the scientific name for which bird?

8. Where in Great Britain has the White-crowned Sparrow become a bit of a pane?

9. What was the auction price paid for a copy of Audubon's *Birds of America* in November 2010 at Sotheby's in London, a world record for a printed book? Was it £5 million, £7 million or £11 million, to the nearest million?

10. Which of the following birds do not exist: Tennessee Warbler, Oklahoma Warbler, Kentucky Warbler, Connecticut Warbler?

11. Who is the Editor of *British Birds*?

12. What is a snood on a Wild Turkey?

13. What is the most numerous seabird breeding in the British Isles?

14. Young of which bird family have the fastest growth in the first three days after hatching?

15. How has the Oriental Turtle Dove helped the European Turtle Dove migrating through Malta this year?

16. Name one of the two eminent ornithologists who wrote *Wild America* in 1953, an account of a three month peregrination round North America?

17. Name the other.

18. Who says in Shakespeare's *Romeo and Juliet* : 'It was the nightingale, and not the lark,/That pierced the fearful hollow of thine ear'?

19. Apart from Prince Ruspoli's Gecko and Prince Ruspoli's Shovel-snout, what other species is named after Prince Ruspoli?

20. Apart from predation by cats and rats, what is the chief threat to the Mascarene Petrel on Réunion?

2011 C
Paul Donald – OBC

Answers: page 257

1. In which UK Overseas Territory does the Henderson Crake breed?

2. In which UK Overseas Territory does the Endangered Atlantic (Schlegel's) Petrel breed?

3. A flock of what species stopped the minute hand of Big Ben in 1949 by roosting upon it?

4. In what way is the nest of Nordmann's Greenshank unusual for a wader?

5. What connects David Graham, George Bristow and Richard Meinertzhagen ornithologically?

6. In what year was the Gannet last seen in Thetford?

7. Which is the most numerous breeding tern in the British Isles?

8. 'Old Blue' was the last fertile female New Zealand Black Robin who helped save the species from extinction. What was the name of her mate?

9. Which of the following birds do not exist: Golden-winged Warbler, Golden-cheeked Warbler, Golden-browed Warbler, Golden-rumped Warbler?

10. What is the name of the project that is supported by Disney's Friends for Change, which protects the Spoon-billed Sandpiper's feeding and resting sites in China?

11. Which playwright wrote *The Birds* in 414 BCE (also *The Frogs* and *The Wasps*)?

12. Do bustards have uropygial or preen glands?

13. Who wrote: 'A robin redbreast in a cage/Puts all heaven in a rage'?

14. What is the journal of Oriental Bird Club called?

15. In which English county was the first *confirmed* record of a Black-browed Albatross (in 1897)?

16. With what does the EU consortium DAISIE concern itself in connection with threats to birds?

17. What do the recently rediscovered Banggai Crow and Large-billed Reed Warbler have in common?

18. Was the Eurasian Collared Dove first recorded in the USA in 1986, 1996 or 2006?

19. What species, first seen and heard at Rye Harbour in Sussex in 1983, has become a new species for Britain following re-splitting?

20. Apart from poisoning and habitat loss through afforestation, what is the chief threat to the Western Cape population of Blue Cranes in South Africa?

2011 D
Oscar Campbell – OSME

Answers: page 258

1. In which UK Overseas Territory is the Montserrat Oriole to be found?

2. In which UK Overseas Territory is the Vulnerable Spectacled Petrel to be found breeding?

3. Which local poet wrote: 'Little trotty wagtail he went in the rain,/And twittering, tottering sideways he ne'er got straight again'?

4. What caused the death of 25 Zino's Petrel chicks (out of a total of 38) in 2010 on Madeira?

5. What bird is known as 'haring ibon' ('king bird') in Tagalog, the Philippine national language, which is why the Haribon Foundation is so called?

6. Name a wader on the British List whose name describes its feeding method, and Killdeer is not acceptable.

7. Name another.

8. What is the name of the marine debris in the North Pacific Gyre from where Laysan Albatrosses on Kure Atoll in Hawaii gather ten times as much plastic debris than the more eastern albatrosses on Oahu?

9. When was the first modern field guide, *A Field Guide to the Birds*, by Roger Tory Peterson published? Was it 1934, 1936 or 1938?

10. What birds produce their characteristic display sounds by 'aeroelastic flutter' between 50 and 86 kph (31–53 mph)?

11. What is cronism?

12. Name one of the two Critically Endangered species endemic to Gough Island that are threatened by House Mice.

13. Name the other.

14. Which of the following birds do not exist: Black-throated Green Warbler, Black-throated Grey Warbler, Black-throated Yellow Warbler, Black-throated Blue Warbler?

15. What sort of bird is described as a musket by a falconer?

16. Which is the most numerous breeding gull in the British Isles?

17. OSME was formed in April 1978 from which ornithological organization?

18. Was bird-trapping in Cyprus more intense in the UK bases or in the Republic in the autumn of 2010?

19. Synanthropy has become a feature of breeding Critically Endangered Sociable Lapwings. What is synanthropy?

20. What taxonomic similarities do the Intermediate Parakeet and Imperial Pheasant share?

2012 A
Andy Clements – BTO

Answers: page 258

1. Apart from Antarctica, name a continent in which the Barn Owl does not breed.

2. What bird is a 'bow' in Cockney rhyming slang?

3. Who wrote: 'The grackle's voice is less than mellow,/his heart is black, his eye is yellow;/He bullies more attractive birds/with hoodlum deeds and vulgar words./And should a human interfere/attacks that human in the rear./I cannot help but deem the grackle/an ornithological debacle'. ?

4. The eggs of which Critically Endangered species were taken by conservationists from Heritage Expeditions' ship *Spirit of Enderby* last year in Anadyr in far eastern Russia?

5. When did the population of Common Whitethroats crash due to a drought in the Sahel?

6. What is the heaviest species of waterfowl?

7. To what wildfowl species was Gisli Oddsson, Bishop of Skálholt in southern Iceland, referring when he noted in 1638 that '... every year in autumn they make for neighbouring countries of England and Ireland and Scotland ...'?

8. Which of the following birds do not exist – Jungle Babbler, Jungle Francolin, Jungle Flycatcher and Jungle Myna?

9. What species of wader successfully hatched young in 2011 and 2012 for the first time in Rutland?

10. Who wrote the classic *Palaearctic-African Bird Migration Systems*, published in 1972?

11. Where else do Twite breed apart from north-west Europe?

12. Which species of penguin was once known as Bearded Penguin?

13. What sort of bird is a Pediunker?

14. Who is the author of *Birds in Leicestershire and Rutland*, published in 1978?

15. What is the most obvious difference between a Bahama Mockingbird and a Tequila Mockingbird?

16. Are there more Snail Kites than Snail-eating Couas in the world?

17. When did Gannets last breed successfully on Lundy? Was it 1885, 1905 or 1925?

18. What seabird species has successfully colonised Midway in the Pacific, and raised a chick, having previously been confined to two small Japanese islands?

19. Name one of the six artists who illustrated the massive *The Handbook of Bird Identification for Europe and the Western Palearctic* by Mark Beaman and Steve Madge.

20. What species was accused by Saudi Arabia of spying, because it had been fitted with a GPS transmitter by Tel Aviv University?

2012 B
Mike Blair – OSME

Answers: page 259

1. Apart from Antarctica, name a continent in which the Barn Swallow does not breed.

2. What sort of bird is a Piapiac?

3. Which conservation organisation celebrated its centenary this year?

4. What percentage of Nazca Boobies on Isla Española in the Galapagos were noted to have lost more than a quarter of one of their feet, presumed to be due to predation by fish while roosting on the sea at night? Was it 4%, 24% or 44%?

5. How many pairs of White-tailed Eagles bred in Scotland in 2010? Was it 32, 42 or 52?

6. What is the heaviest species of hummingbird?

7. Which of the following birds do not exist – Citrine Wagtail, Citrine Warbler, Citrine Fruit-crow and Citrine Pygmy Parrot?

8. On average, how many feathers does a Great Crested Grebe have in its stomach at any one time (to protect it from sharp fish bones), give or take 20?

9. Who wrote *Where to Watch Birds*, published in 1967 – the first site guide for British birds?

10. What length of shelf space do the 16 volumes of *The Handbook of Birds of the World* take?

11. What Jamaican bird is known as 'Blue Baize', 'Swee', 'Long-month Bluequit', 'Bluebird', 'Blue Badas' and 'Blue Gay'?

12. Which species of penguin was once known as Grand Penguin?

13. What bird is referred to in the title of Beethoven's 'Kakadu Variations' ('Ich bin der Schneider Kakadu')?

14. Who is the editor of *World Birdwatch* magazine?

15. What species of wader visited Rutland Water on 13th April 2012 – the first Rutland record (and last seen in Leicestershire in 1987)?

16. Name one of the two UK Overseas Territories, which are World Heritage Sites, that are or were in danger of being blacklisted by UNESCO due to rats and mice that are threatening much of their avifauna with extinction?

17. The African Bird Club Conservation Fund passed a milestone of money raised this year? How much money has been raised?

18. How many species of cormorant occur in New Zealand, give or take two?

19. What is the most abundant breeding seabird on Lundy?

20. With which scarce British wetlandbird was Emma Turner associated in the first part of the 20th century, providing the first photographic evidence of its return to Britain as a breeding bird in Norfolk in 1911?

2012 C
Graham Madge – OBC

Answers: page 259

1. Apart from Antarctica, name a continent in which the Black-crowned Night Heron does not breed.

2. How many Ivory-billed Woodpeckers have been ringed in the USA?

3. Are there more species of cormorant in the northern or southern hemisphere?

4. Which species of *Hippolais* warbler has bred in Britain?

5. Who illustrated *Birds of Europe with North Africa and the Middle East* by Lars Jonsson?

6. Which of the following birds do not exist – Moreau's Sunbird, Mrs Moreau's Warbler, Gould's Warbler or Mrs Gould's Sunbird?

7. What is the heaviest seabird?

8. What is the very topical subspecific name of the *race* of (White-throated) Dipper that occurred in Cyprus, although it is now extinct?

9. Which is the only country that has two BirdLife partners?

10. What is the population of the Antarctic Prion on South Georgia, to the nearest 5 million pairs?

11. What killed Rutland Water's American Wigeon on 28th November 2011?

12. In Shakespeare's *Henry IV Part I*, what bird did Hotspur propose to teach to say the word 'Mortimer' in order to disturb Henry IV's sleep?

13. Jan Tinbergen was awarded the Nobel Prize for Economics in 1969. For what did brother Niko also win a Nobel Prize?

14. What sort of bird is a Pardusco?

15. When was the Leicestershire and Rutland Wildlife Trust founded? Was it 1936, 1946 or 1956?

16. What was the average speed that the fastest of three Great Snipe fitted with geolocators in Sweden travelled to Central Africa in 2010? Was it 86, 96 or 106 kph?

17. How many twitchers managed to see the Common Nighthawk at Horden, Co Durham, on 11th October 2010?

18. What was the fate of an Amur Falcon, rescued in May 1984 in Aquitaine and rehabilitated and released, which was subsequently hit by a car in Easingwold, Yorkshire, whence, after recovering, it was released again later in 1984?

19. Name one of the three artists whose illustrations were used in both the first (1968–72) Atlas of Breeding Birds of Britain and Ireland and the second (New) (1988–91) Atlas.

20. Who is the author of *The Birds of Rutland and its Reservoirs*, published in 1984?

2012 D
John Clark – ABC

Answers: page 259

1. Apart from Antarctica, name a continent in which the Common Moorhen does not breed.

2. Were there more young Spoonbills or young Spoon-billed Sandpipers in Britain in 2011?

3. What bird did Chairman Mao try to exterminate in 1958 as part of the Four Pests Campaign in the Great Leap Forward, by getting the Chinese to disturb them continuously so they could not land to feed (and also by other methods)?

4. What is the heaviest species of bustard?

5. When does the shooting season for Red Grouse end?

6. What unusual feature do the tail feathers of the Onagadori rooster possess?

7. What is the only passerine that breeds on South Georgia?

8. Which Eastern Palaearctic raptor of wild origin was first recorded in Britain in 2008?

9. When did Kentish Plovers last nest successfully in England? Was it 1939, 1959 or 1979?

10. Which of the following birds do not exist – Bonaparte's Gull, Josephine's Lorikeet, Nelson's Sparrow or Hamilton's Thrasher?

11. Which distinguished ornithologist and author and former editor of *British Birds* celebrated his 100th birthday on 9th June 2012?

12. Which famous classical composer had a pet starling that could sing part of his Piano Concerto No. 17 in G Major (Köchel number 453)?

13. Name one of the two artists who illustrated *Collins Bird Guide* by Lars Svensson and Peter Grant (published in 1999).

14. Name one of the constituents of a Yellow Parrot cocktail.

15. Which species of penguin was once known as Victoria Penguin?

16. Name one of the novel ways that the Sharp-beaked Ground Finch on Wolf Island in the Galapagos obtains food from Nazca Boobies

17. Which subspecies of Cackling Goose was thought to be extinct until its rediscovery in 1962 and now has a population of about 100,000 birds?

18. How much did Yorkshire Naturalist Trust (now Wildlife Trust) pay for Spurn Head Nature Reserve in 1959? Was it £150, £1,500 or £15,000?

19. Name one of the authors of *The Birds of Leicestershire and Rutland*, published in 2009.

20. Who is the editor of *Birdwatch* magazine?

2013 A
Jonathan Meyrav – OSME

Answers: page 260

1. What is the world population of the Alaotra Grebe believed to be?

2. Which species nested successfully for the first time in Britain in Shapwick Heath in 2012?

3. Which British species is most frequently infected with avian pox?

4. Of which football club is Cyril the Swan the mascot?

5. Where does Kirtland's Warbler winter?

6. Which Near Threatened species comprises nearly one-third of the diet of feral cats on Le Levant island off the south of France?

7. Whose 83rd symphony is known as 'The Hen'?

8. What unusual food (for a sandpiper) forms a large part of the diet of the Tuamotu Sandpiper?

9. Which of the following birds do not exist: Golden-crowned Manakin, Golden-headed Manakin, Golden-rumped Manakin, Golden-collared Manakin?

10. The Madeiran Storm-petrel has now been split into three species – Madeiran, Cape Verde and Monteiro's Storm-petrels. Which one rejoices in the scientific name *Oceanodroma jabejabe*?

11. What was the name of the census of breeding seabirds in Britain and Ireland in 1969–70?

12. Who was the International Council for Bird Preservation's first General Secretary for 43 years from 1935 to 1978 (for which she was unpaid)?

13. What unusual trend happened to the Falkland Islands' Black-browed Albatross population between 2005 and 2010?

14. Why is the Robust Woodpecker more robust than the Robust Crow and the Robust Elephant-bird?

15. What is the connection between Jeffrey Archer and the Liben Lark?

16. What species was almost certainly finally exterminated from Auckland Island, New Zealand, by intense collecting for the British Museum in 1901 and 1902?

17. Barba Azul grassland reserve in Bolivia was created because of its importance for the Critically Endangered Blue-throated Macaw, but for which trans-continental migrant is it also crucial?

18. Which English county formerly had the most duck decoys?

19. How many Osprey chicks were translocated to Rutland for the Rutland Water Osprey project? Was it 50, 75 or 100?

20. How many species of Critically Endangered vulture breed in India?

2013 B
Adam Riley – ABC

Answers: page 260

1. What is the world population of the Atitlan Grebe believed to be?

2. Three species of petrel are named after people who travelled on the *Endeavour* on Captain Cook's first circumnavigation of the world. Name one.

3. What dull bird is the national bird of Costa Rica?

4. What is the collective noun for herons?

5. What species, which had only been recorded once in Britain until a month ago, now breeds again on the island after which it is named?

6. Which of the following birds do not exist: Red-throated Tanager, Rose-throated Tanager, Rusty-throated Tanager, Rufous-throated Tanager?

7. When was the Short-toed Treecreeper first recorded in England?

8. What particular threats do Dickcissels and Bobolinks face in their huge traditional roosts in the Venezuelan part of the Llanos?

9. On how many BTO Garden Bird Feeding Survey bird-tables were Cormorants recorded feeding last winter?

10. Which European woodpecker also breeds in North America?

11. What is the name of the boat that takes people on Osprey-watching cruises on Rutland Water?

12. What was the name of Dr Dolittle's parrot?

13. Name one of the states where Kirtland's Warbler breeds.

14. Which species of falcon was recently found being caught for the pot in huge numbers on migration, by mist-netting in Nagaland in north-east India?

15. At which London sporting venue did Lesser Black-backed Gulls start breeding in 1982?

16. Which occurred first – the first Birdfair or ICBP becoming BirdLife International?

17. Guatemala's second city is, arguably, named after which spectacular bird, which is also Guatemala's national bird?

18. Apart from the USA, in which country has the California Condor bred in the wild following its reintroduction?

19. The French call a nocturnal African bird *Engoulevent à balanciers*. What do we call it?

20. Who wrote the lines: 'He thought he saw an Albatross that fluttered round the lamp – He looked again and found it was a Penny-Postage Stamp'?

2013 C
Adrian Pitches – OBC

Answers: page 260

1. What is the world population of the Colombian (Tota) Grebe believed to be?

2. Which is the only Critically Endangered species to be seen regularly in Britain?

3. In which decade were Great Tits first observed opening milk bottle tops?

4. What was the agricultural pesticide, introduced in the late 1940s, that caused a catastrophic decline in the populations of many raptors due to egg-shell thinning?

5. What sort of poison was one of the main causes of the near-extinction of the Californian Condor and is still a threat affecting about 20% of the population?

6. Which bird family contains the largest number of Critically Endangered species?

7. Who is the editor of *Birdwatching* magazine?

8. Name one of the three *(four)* Directors/CEOs of ICBP/ BirdLife since 1980.

9. How many species of tanager does *The Handbook of Birds of the World* recognise?

10. Name one of the two species on the British List that have the letter 'J' in their generic name.

11. Prior to 2011 only one British-ringed Cuckoo had been recovered in Africa when a bird was taken for the pot. In which country was it caught?

12. What bird species has been a serious threat to Kirtland's Warbler?

13. On which island/archipelago would you have looked for a Stumbling Moa-nalo before it became extinct?

14. According to a recent survey by BirdLife Cyprus, how many birds were killed in Cyprus by trapping with mist-nets and lime-sticks in 2011? Was it 28,000, 280,000 or 2,800,000?

15. Which rare bird in Great Britain had 29 records in 2011, which exactly matched all previous records?

16. What adaptation do male Sungrebes have for carrying their altricial young, which is unique among birds?

17. Although Miguel Alvarez del Toro discovered this in 1970, who had actually written about it in 1822 but was ignored or disbelieved?

18. In which year did Ospreys first breed in Rutland?

19. Who wrote in 1950 in the BTO's *How to Choose and Use Field-glasses*, 'It is evident to anyone who glances at a party of ornithologists trying to use telescopes on a mud-flat that sooner or later either the telescope or the birdwatcher will have to be redesigned. The former would be more convenient'?

20. Marmora's Warbler has been split into Marmora's and Balearic Warbler. What is the scientific name of the Balearic Warbler?

2013 D
Andy Musgrove – BTO

Answers: page 261

1. What is the world population of the Labrador Duck believed to be?

2. A Sanderling trapped by the Wash Wader Ringing Group in August 2012 had been ringed previously in which land-locked country?

3. What alternative name do Wryneck and Anhinga share?

4. Pandemonium is the collective noun for birds of which family?

5. What years did the first Atlas of Breeding Birds of Britain and Ireland cover?

6. How many 10 km squares had confirmed breeding Red-backed Shrikes in the 1968–72 Atlas survey?

7. Which is faster – a White-throated Needletail (arguably the fastest bird in the world) or the blade of a wind-turbine on Harris?

8. Nathan Leopold was considered to be the leading expert on Kirtland's Warbler in the 1920s. Why was he unable to continue his study of the bird between 1924 and 1957?

9. The range of which species is considered to be restricted by a 'climate bubble of less than 20°C' in southern Ethiopia?

10. What recently rediscovered bird has been found to be breeding on Little Barrier Island in New Zealand?

11. In the novel *Bird Brain* by Guy Kennaway, as what bird was Basil 'Banger' Peyton-Crumbe reincarnated after his unfortunate murder?

12. Which of the following birds do not exist: Yellow-necked Tanager, Yellow-scarfed Tanager, Yellow-throated Tanager, Yellow-crested Tanager?

13. What trivial masticatory use of PIB (Polyisobutene), which was responsible for the January 2013 seabird wreck off the south coast, was highlighted by the newspapers and respected ornithological journals such as *British Birds*?

14. Lance Richdale carried out famous studies on two iconic New Zealand species from 1936 onwards. Name one.

15. Which Critically Endangered duck, which has not been seen by Tim Appleton, was only considered to be Vulnerable as recently as 2007?

16. What island in the Seychelles archipelago was purchased by ICBP *(now BirdLife)* in 1968 to help save the Seychelles Warbler (inter alia)?

17. Up to 2012 how many Osprey chicks had fledged in Rutland? Was it 52, 62 or 72?

18. What bird do the Australian aborigines call 'The Rain Brother'?

19. The French call a nocturnal African bird *Engoulevent porte-étendard*. What do we call it?

20. In 1913 what had once been Haggerstone Entomological Society and Clapton Naturalists' Field Club united to become which organization?

2014 A
Neil Calbrade – BTO

Answers: page 261

1. What is the largest species of bustard on the BOU's British List?

2. In the nursery rhyme 'Sing a Song of Sixpence' (2.4 new pence), how many Blackbirds were baked in a pie?

3. Before it was called *Birds* and now *Nature's Home*, what was the RSPB magazine called?

4. What sad event occurred 100 years ago on 1st September 1914 (in Cincinnati)?

5. Were more 75 year old men or 75 year old women unable to hear a Goldcrest's song in a recent survey?

6. Who is the President of the RSPB?

7. Spell her name.

8. Which of the following birds do not exist: Black-capped Siskin, Black-chinned Siskin, Black-headed Siskin, Black-eared Siskin?

9. Which group of birds are especially threatened by the parasitic fly *Philornis downsi*?

10. Who has painted 23 of the 26 front cover illustrations of the Birdfair programme since 1989?

11. According to the 2007–11 Atlas, at how many Gannet

colonies in Britain and Ireland was there confirmed breeding? Was it 26, 28 or 30?

12. Name one of the species of albatross that have been down-listed on the IUCN Red List due to the results of efforts to reduce bycatch in long-line fisheries.

13. Which European country has the highest breeding population of White Storks?

14. In which European country has a 34 million year old fossil ancestor of the Hoatzin recently been found?

15. Which organization was the first to receive funding from the proceeds of the 'Champions of the Flyway' bird race held in Israel this year?

16. What colour are owls' eggs?

17. How many twitchers saw the Dusky Thrush in Leigh, Greater Manchester, on 8th December 2010?

18. What 50 year old bird was recently recovered in Lake Bogoria in Kenya?

19. What species is 'Moonbird', or B95, who has a statue in Mispillion Harbor in Delaware, in honour of 400,000 miles of migration over 19 years to Tierra del Fuego and back?

20. Were Reed Buntings or Yellowhammers confirmed to be breeding in more 10 km squares in Britain in the 2007–11 *Atlas*?

2014 B
Nick Acheson – OSME

Answers: page 261

1. What is the largest auk still on the BOU's British List?

2. When did Sir Peter Scott start recording the individual bill patterns of Bewick's Swans at Slimbridge? Was it 1960, 1964 or 1968?

3. Where have BirdLife and other agencies been successful in stopping the horrendous slaughter of migrating Amur Falcons?

4. What species of guineafowl are domesticated?

5. How many volumes comprise *Birds of the Western Palaearctic*, edited by Cramp *et al.*, published between 1977 and 1992?

6. What did George Ligowsky of Cincinnati invent in 1880 as a result of the rapidly declining population of the Passenger Pigeon?

7. Which North American woodpecker of Red-bellied Woodpecker, Red-headed Woodpecker and Red-cockaded Woodpecker has the least amount of red on the head in all adult plumages?

8. Which British wader, previously presumed to winter in the Middle East with its European congeners, caused some surprise in 2013 by migrating to Peru via Greenland and Mexico, when tracked by geolocator?

9. Which of the following birds do not exist: King Rail, King Quail, King Whydah, King Eider?

10. What is the only endemic bird species to survive on Bermuda, thanks to man's depredations?

11. What is unusual about the diet of the Atoll Fruit-dove?

12. Who painted the first two front cover illustrations of the Birdfair programme?

13. How many foveas do raptors have in each eye?

14. What is unusual about the relationship between African Tigerfish and Barn Swallows in Mapungubwe National Park in South Africa?

15. In how many European countries does the White-headed Duck now breed?

16. Name one of the Bird Observatories in Britain accredited to the Bird Observatories Council, which is currently active, which shares its name with one of the sea areas named in the shipping forecast of the BBC.

17. Were Dippers or Kingfishers confirmed to be breeding in more 10 km squares in Britain in the 2007–11 Atlas?

18. In which country is the most northerly breeding colony of Spoonbills in Europe?

19. What is a Welsh Partridge?

20. Which African country has the most Globally Threatened species?

2014 C
Callan Cohen – ABC

Answers: page 262

1. What is the largest owl on the BOU's British List?

2. In which English island have breeding Manx Shearwaters increased tenfold in 10 years since the eradication of rats in 2002?

3. Which drug have the veterinary authorities in Spain and Italy allowed for use in domestic animals, despite its known devastating effect on vultures?

4. How many volumes comprise the *Handbook of Birds of the World*, edited by Josep del Hoyo, published between 1992 and 2011 (excluding the Special Volume published in 2013)?

5. What percentage of its Biodiversity Conservation Budget does Defra spend on the UK Overseas Territories, with their 32 Threatened species?

6. Which British bird of prey has the longest incubation period at 43–45 days?

7. Which goose species had a breeding population in the Netherlands of one pair in 1967 and almost 5,000 pairs in 2000?

8. Which widespread woodlandbird was first recorded breeding in Scotland in 1989?

9. Which of the following birds do not exist: Gibberbird, Babbler, Chatterer, Blatherer?

10. In which month have more than half of the North American landbirds in Britain been discovered?

11. In the nest of which African bird was found 100 kg of grass, a plastic dish, two socks, a glove, a comb, a leather belt, a pair of men's underpants, six bicycle tyres, six pieces of asbestos roofing, seven bits of hosepipe and 186 other anthropogenic items?

12. Apart from Pheasant, what is the only British non-passerine to have a breeding population in excess of a million pairs?

13. What is the collective noun for storks?

14. The name of the last Passenger Pigeon was Martha, supposedly after the wife of the first President of the USA, but what was the name of the last male (who died in 1909)?

15. What was the species that *British Birds* warned its readers to be aware of in March 1958, as some had recently escaped from captivity and had been confused with its rare European relative?

16. Richard Burton, Roger Moore and Richard Harris starred in which film with an ornithological title?

17. Which European country has the highest breeding population of Lesser Kestrels?

18. Which is the only country in West Africa where Lesser Flamingos have successfully bred?

19. Were Greylag Geese or Canada Geese confirmed to be breeding in more 10 km squares in Britain in the 2007–11 Atlas?

20. Which is the only species to have appeared on the front cover illustrations of the Birdfair programme more than once – three times in fact?

2014 D
Chris Gooddie – OBC

Answers: page 262

1. What is the biggest tit on the BOU's British List?

2. Name one of the four countries with more than 100 Globally Threatened bird species.

3. How many volumes comprise the *Handbook of British Birds*, by Witherby, Jourdain, Ticehurst and Tucker, published in 1940?

4. Which of the following birds do not exist: Red Lory, Yellow-billed Lory, Red Lorikeet, Yellow-billed Lorikeet?

5. How many species of albatross are protected by the Agreement on the Conservation of Albatrosses and Petrels (ACAP)?

6. The future for which species of vulture looks brighter since the Sudanese government switched off the power in the notorious power line from Port Sudan to the Red Sea coast, which had previously electrocuted large numbers?

7. Which is the only part of Greece where the Lammergeier now breeds, following its extirpation from the rest of the country?

8. Name the only native all white wildfowl in the southern hemisphere.

9. Why is the Thrush Nightingale known as the Sprosser?

10. What caused the disturbance that led to six pairs of Northen Bald Ibis at Souss Massa National Park failing to raise young in 2013 in what was otherwise a bumper year for the species?

11. Which species of albatross was believed to be extinct in 1949 until it was rediscovered in 1951?

12. Where outside New Zealand is the world's largest kiwi to be found?

13. Which was founded first – the National Audubon Society or the (Royal) Society for the Protection of Birds?

14. Which distinguished ornithologist's most memorable piece of advice is 'if you hear a call and you don't recognise it – it's a Great Tit'?

15. How do the eyes of Skimmers differ from those of all other birds?

16. Which species has colonised Ireland since the 1988–91 Atlas?

17. Were Treecreepers or Nuthatches confirmed to be breeding in more 10 km squares in Britain in the 2007–11 Atlas?

18. What is the collective noun for flamingos?

19. Name one of the two non-native species of passerine that has bred in the wild in the British Isles since 1996.

20. Name one of the two species that comprise 60% of the spring records of North American landbirds in Britain?

2015 A
Fiona Barclay – BTO

Answers: page 262

1. In which country would you look for Sakalava Rail, Red-shouldered Vanga and Madagascar Fish-eagle?

2. What adjective can describe a tit, a warbler, a harrier and a sandpiper on the British List?

3. Which unsuccessful contestant for Bird Brain of Britain in 2002 and 2003 was one of the first to rediscover the Zapata Rail in November 2014?

4. Which vertebrate is the most abundant in the diet of Honey-buzzards breeding in the UK?

5. What is the longest partnership of Bewick's Swans recorded at Slimbridge? Was it 11, 16 or 21 years?

6. What was novel about the record of White's Thrush at Spinningdale in the Highlands on 31st January 2013?

7. Although the judges chose Edmund Fellowes's Grey Heron as Bird Photograph of the Year 2014, what photograph did Birdfair visitors to the *British Birds* stand select?

8. How many times has the Loch Garten Ospreys' nesting tree been cut down by vandals?

9. When was the last Little Bustard shot in England?

10. Which of the following does not exist: Jerdon's Courser, Jerdon's Baza, Jerdon's Nightjar, Jerdon's Pitta?

11. Which species of hummingbird, endemic to the Santa Marta Mountains of Colombia and unseen since 1946, was rediscovered in March 2015?

12. Which species was scientifically described first – Marsh Tit or Willow Tit?

13. Bigua, Brazilian, Mexican and Olivaceous are descriptive adjectives formerly used for which widespread neotropical bird?

14. What caused the death of 25 juvenile and 3 adult Zino's Petrels in Madeira in August 2010?

15. Which Estonian ornithologist had his portrait on the 2 kroon banknote and also has a Critically Endangered duck named after him?

16. Which passerine species had ceased to breed in Ireland between the 1988–91 Atlas and the 2007–11 Atlas?

17. What species of penguin is 'Tango' in the children's book *And Tango Makes Three*, a book banned in many American libraries because it was interpreted by some as trying to spread the Gay Rights message?

18. One definite and two possibly extinct birds have been depicted on the front cover illustrations of the Birdfair programme. Name one.

19. Which Hawaiian island has the Hawaiian Goose recolonised, of its own volition, in addition to Hawaii, Maui, Molokai and Kauai?

20. Who wrote *One Flew into the Cuckoo's Egg*, published in 2008?

2015 B
Tom Lewis – ABC

Answers: page 263

1. In which country would you look for Crow Honeyeater, Kagu and New Caledonia Rail?

2. What species was the late Bowland Betty?

3. What waterbird entered the front door of 10 Downing Street, which had been left open in the hot weather on 28th May this year?

4. Name one of the two species of cormorant used to catch fish in China and Japan.

5. What is the only species of penguin named after a French woman?

6. Which was the first Bird Observatory to be established in Britain (in 1933)?

7. Which of the following does not exist: Salvadori's Courser, Salvadori's Nightjar, Salvadori's Pheasant, Salvadori's Teal?

8. Which species was scientifically described first – Emperor Penguin or Emperor Goose?

9. Where would you find a bird's pecten?

10. What adjective can describe a dove, a flycatcher and a pratincole on the British List?

11. For what supposed properties are Golden Orioles particularly prized by hunters in the Eastern Mediterranean?

12. How much money have the manufacturers of diclofenac contributed to the costs of breeding India's vultures in captivity?

13. In the nursery rhyme 'Sing a Song of Sixpence', what facial mutilation was inflicted by the Blackbird on the maid as she was hanging out the clothes?

14. For how many years has trapping of songbirds in Cyprus been illegal? Is it 20, 30 or 40 years?

15. What is the chief threat to the Cape Verde Shearwater?

16. In which British military base were an estimated 900,000 songbirds killed in autumn 2014?

17. How many of the world's 12,000 Important Bird and Biodiversity Areas (IBAs) are in imminent danger of being lost, according to BirdLife International? Is it 356, 456 or 556?

18. Of BirdLife's 120 partners, how many have logos with no recognizable bird depicted on them? Is it 10, 30 or 50?

19. Although Red-flanked Bluetail was first recorded in Great Britain in 1903, in which decade was it first recorded in Ireland?

20. Did Montagu's Harriers in England fledge more young in 2013 or 2014?

2015 C
Tom McKinney – OSME

Answers: page 263

1. In which country would you look for Fernandina's Flicker, Zapata Rail and Cuban Parakeet?

2. Name two of the three principal species that produce guano on the Chincha Islands off Peru.

3. What was the species whose nine nest histories in 1939 resulted in the BTO's Nest Record Scheme?

4. What remarkable feature was shown in a photograph of a female Critically Endangered Mascerene Petrel taken by Hadoram Shirihai off Réunion last year?

5. Do the Chinese have a Birdfair?

6. Which is the only state of the USA where Wild Turkeys do not now occur?

7. Is the Passenger Pigeon chewing louse *Colombicola extinctus* extinct?

8. Name two bird species that have been recorded killing Rose-ringed Parakeets in London parks.

9. From which country, with a dubious record of adherence to the EU Birds Directive, does Karmenu Vella, the European Commissioner for the Environment and Fisheries hail?

10. What does the word Tapaculo literally mean in Spanish?

11. Which of the following does not exist: Hartlaub's Bustard, Hartlaub's Gull, Hartlaub's Nightjar, Hartlaub's Turaco?

12. How many times have vandals burned down the hide at the Loch Garten Osprey site?

13. What adjective can describe a warbler, a tern, a skua and a redpoll on the British List?

14. What was the estimated number of calling Corncrakes on the Nene Washes in 2014? Was it 22, 33 or 44?

15. Which species was scientifically described first – Whooper Swan or Bewick's/Tundra Swan?

16. According to Simon Barnes, how much money is estimated to be earned for the economy of Mull by the two eagle species that occur there?

17. The ex-gamekeeper at the Stody Estate in Norfolk received a ten week suspended sentence in November 2014 for poisoning nine birds of which species?

18. Which was the most recent Bird Observatory to be accredited by the Bird Observatories Council (in 2002)?

19. How many thrushes in the genus *Turdus* are on the British List – give or take one?

20. What was the first non-European bird to appear on the front cover illustrations of the Birdfair programme in 1994, when Halmahera was the project?

2015 D
Stuart Elsom – OBC

Answers: page 263

1. In which country would you look for Bannerman's Turaco, Mount Kupe Bush-shrike and Mount Cameroon Francolin?

2. What species of bird is Chris, who has migrated from East Anglia to the Congo for the last four years, bearing a tag?

3. How many of the 125 Red-eyed Vireos found in Britain up to 2012 were first discovered in the months of September, October and November?

4. How many kilometres of mist-nets were deployed on Egypt's north coast in 2012 by hunters to catch migrant birds? Was it 7, 70 or 700 kms?

5. How many pheasants are released for shooting purposes each year in Britain, to the nearest 5 million?

6. Which English county formerly had the most duck decoys?

7. Which of the following megapodes is not extinct – Pit-builder Megapode, Noble Megapode, Nicobar Megapode, Consumed Megapode?

8. Name one of the two Scilly Isles where Manx Shearwater chicks have avoided the depredation by rats for the first time for many decades, following rat eradication.

9. In which part of its range has the population of Houbara Bustard increased in the last 30 years without the aid of artificially reared reintroduced birds?

10. Statistically, on what day in mid October are you most likely to see a North American landbird in the UK?

11. In which book are flamingos used as croquet mallets?

12. What depressing decision did the Maltese people take on 11th April 2015?

13. What adjective can describe a grebe, a nightjar, a stint and a phalarope on the British List?

14. Who painted the 2004 front cover illustration of the Birdfair programme, which depicts an Amazilia Hummingbird and a Tropical Parula mobbing a tree snake in the Tumbesian region of Peru and Ecuador?

15. Which species was scientifically described first – Sabine's Gull or Ross's Gull?

16. How many booming Bitterns were confirmed in the UK in 2014? Was it 120, 140 or 160?

17. What was the chief beneficiary of the Champions of the Flyway 2015 bird race?

18. What age was the oldest Little Tern to be recovered in Britain? Was it nearly 16, 19 or 22 years?

19. Who wrote *Cuckoos, Cowbirds and Other Cheats*, published in 2000?

20. What cryptic species was discovered in Brazil in 2002, but has not been seen or heard since?

2016 A
Stephen McAvoy – BTO

Answers: page 264

1. *Podiceps cristatus* is the Latin name for which breeding British bird?

2. What is the usual clutch size of the Lesser Black-backed Gull?

3. What type of bird is a Snowcap?

4. Which species of seabird do the owners of Vermont Hotel in Newcastle controversially seek to prevent breeding on the Tyne Bridge 'in order to create a safer and more hygienic area for pedestrians'?

5. Which lays the larger egg – Great Spotted Kiwi or Emu?

6. For which species was Peter Scott searching successfully in 1946 at Slimbridge, which inspired him to found the Wildfowl Trust there?

7. Which Australian pigeon shares its name with a British pay-day loans company?

8. When were satellite tags first fitted to British Cuckoos?

9. Which of the following species does not exist: Spot-backed Antpitta, Spot-backed Antbird, Spot-backed Antshrike or Spot-backed Antwren?

10. What fate befell the first male Guadalcanal Moustached Kingfisher to be mist-netted in the Solomon Islands in 2015?

11. According to Pliny, how did the Greek dramatist Aeschylus die?

12. Who, until April 2015, was the President of the British Ornithologists' Union?

13. Which sex generally incubates the eggs of the Dotterel?

14. What colour is the throat of a (Bohemian) Waxwing?

15. Birds of which genus may be Laughing, Spangled or Blue-winged?

16. Who wrote *Evenings at The Coot and Corncrake – A Birdwatcher's Quiz Book* in 1986 (and was subsequently crowned Bird Brain of Britain on four occasions)?

17. The extinction of which species was finally accomplished by Sigurdur Isleifsson, Ketil Ketilsson and Jon Brandsson?

18. Thoth, the ancient Egyptian god of wisdom, is usually depicted having the head of which bird?

19. Which European gull is no longer considered to be Threatened?

20. Richardson's Skua is a former name of which skua?

2016 B
John Kinghorn – ABC

Answers: page 264

1. *Platalea leucorodia* is the Latin name for which breeding British bird?

2. Do Twite breed in Wales?

3. What colour are the legs of a Terek Sandpiper?

4. In which county is Landguard Bird Observatory?

5. Which of the following African vultures are now Critically Endangered – Hooded, Ruppell's, White-backed and White-headed Vulture?

6. In which football ground did a pair of Peregrines nest in 2015 despite several rugby World Cup matches being played with crowds of 30,000?

7. Which football ground lays claim to an earlier nesting of Peregrines in their stand?

8. What type of bird is a Great Argus?

9. Which of the following species does not exist: Silver-backed Tanager, Silver-beaked Tanager, Silver-capped Tanager or Silver-throated Tanager?

10. What birds may be Scarlet, Sacred, Wattled and Hadada?

11. Apart from American Redstart, name one of the two New World warblers on the British List that are named after a place.

12. What is the usual clutch size of the Little Ringed Plover?

13. Which of Rossini's operas concerns a kleptomaniac corvid?

14. Which sex incubates the eggs of the Ruff?

15. Why did the New Brunswick Game Department close the American Woodcock hunting season in 1970?

16. Which is the only species classified as Extinct in the Wild (not just Possibly Extinct in the Wild) that is not an island species?

17. What nationality was Professor Edgardo Moltoni, after whom Moltoni's Warbler is named?

18. Name one of the six species that have been ringed in South Africa and recovered in Britain?

19. Who wrote *The Cuckoo's Secret*, published in 1922?

20. What bird was involved in the destruction of two model aeroplanes in a park in South Bay, Los Angeles, in January 2015, as reported in many British newspapers?

2016 C
Ashley Banwell – OBC

Answers: page 264

1. *Riparia riparia* is the Latin name for which breeding British bird?

2. What mammal was photographed on the back of a flying male Green Woodpecker in Hornchurch in Essex last year?

3. What type of bird is a Sungrebe?

4. What is the usual clutch size of the Common Guillemot?

5. Which is the only *Phylloscopus* warbler regularly to breed in North America?

6. How many nests of Common Eider are required to produce a pound of eiderdown, to the nearest ten nests?

7. Which of the following species does not exist: Black-capped Petrel, Black-winged Petrel, Black-vented Petrel and Black Petrel?

8. What colour is the lower mandible of the male Common Kingfisher?

9. What prevents the Mountain Chicken from flying?

10. Which sex incubates the eggs of the Maleo of Sulawesi?

11. Lady Jane, who died at Cincinnati Zoo in 1917, was the penultimate member of which species (the ultimate member, Incas, died the following year)?

12. Which came first – Penguin Books or Pelican Books?

13. The Bonn Convention of 1983 is concerned with what aspect of bird (and other wild animal) behaviour?

14. What birds may be Black, Painted, Milky and Jabiru?

15. The population of which warbler species on the Seychelles has increased from 26 individuals in 1959 to over 3,000 now, as a result of conservation measures including translocations to other islands within the archipelago?

16. A male of which rare falcon species was shot and killed in Cambridgeshire in 2015 after spending a month outside a Staffordshire colliery?

17. Which species classified as Possibly Extinct in the Wild has recently been seen in Brazil?

18. Why did Joseph Muscat, Prime Minister of Malta, close the spring hunting season early last year?

19. What is the status of the St Helena Hoopoe?

20. The stomachs of dead Puffins on the Isle of May have been found to contain nurdles – the latest ocean pollutant. What are nurdles?

2016 D
Yoav Perlman – OSME

Answers: page 265

1. *Anas strepera* is the Latin name for which breeding British bird?

2. Who was the Atlas Co-ordinator for the 2007–11 Bird Atlas?

3. What is the usual clutch size of hummingbirds?

4. The Latin name of the Inambari Gnatcatcher honours which famous living naturalist?

5. What type of bird is a Luzon Bleeding-heart?

6. Which of the following species does not exist: Striped Sparrow, Three-striped Sparrow, Five-striped Sparrow or Black-striped Sparrow?

7. What colour are a Cetti's Warbler legs?

8. Which previously Near Threatened species of hornbill is now Critically Endangered due to over-exploitation for its ivory-like casque?

9. Despite the fact that lead shot poisons many thousands of wildfowl in Britain each year, what is the tonnage of lead shot still used per year in Britain? Is it 20 tonnes, 200 tonnes or 2,000 tonnes?

10. Which sex incubates Ostrich eggs at night?

11. Name one of the two species of Honeyguide that are not confined to Africa.

12. Two pairs of White-winged Diuca-finch were found nesting in 2014 at what surprising sort of nest site, more usually associated with Emperor Penguins?

13. What proportion of Bewick's Swans winter in East Asia rather than Europe?

14. What does the Akun Eagle-owl eat?

15. What introduced Asian passerine is causing problems by predating seabird eggs on oceanic islands, especially in the Seychelles?

16. Where do you find todies?

17. What brought down at least 43 Common Buzzards in Exeter city centre between 2012 and 2015?

18. What birds may be Pygmy, Double-crested, Flightless and Guanay?

19. With the conservation of which Critically Endangered species is Robert Porter Allen chiefly associated?

20. Who wrote *Fleas, Flukes and Cuckoos*, published in 1952?

2017 A
Ashley Banwell – OBC

Answers: page 265

1. What happened to the last pair of Peregrines that nested in Malta in the last century in 1982?

2. Bifasciated Lark is the old name for which species?

3. What was the occupation of Francesco Cetti, after whom Cetti's Warbler is named?

4. Why did climmers/egg-collectors throw the first-laid guillemot eggs off the cliffs at Bempton in the 19th century when they harvested them?

5. Do more pairs of Chough nest in England, Wales, Scotland or the Isle of Man?

6. Which of the following birds do not exist: Stripe-backed Wren, Stripe-breasted Wren, Stripe-crowned Wren, Stripe-throated Wren?

7. Who was the only female President of the BTO?

8. In which island or archipelago might you expect to see Forest Rock Thrush, Grey Emutail, Sakalava Rail and Red-shouldered Vanga?

9. Which species of heron was first seen in Britain in Norfolk in 2004 and has now been added to the British List following the sighting of a bird in Kent in 2014?

10. What Germans come to British gardens in winter while

the Brits go to Spain and North Africa?

11. How do you spell Pfrimer's Parakeet?

12. What birds may be Sulphur-bellied, Chestnut-bellied, Velvet-fronted, Algerian or Krueper's?

13. What is the most common cause of death of African vultures?

14. What value has BirdLife placed upon each of these poisoned African vultures for their 'cleaning services' e.g., preventing the spread of disease? Is it $110, $1,100 or $11,000?

15. Is the population of Critically Endangered Hooded Grebe 40 pairs, 400 pairs or 4,000 pairs?

16. What is considered to be the main threat to the continued existence of the Chatham Parakeet on three small islands in the Chatham archipelago?

17. Which Asian species, previously of Least Concern, has now been split into 12 species, four of which are either Vulnerable or Endangered?

18. In which archipelago do nearly half of the world population of Southern Giant Petrel breed?

19. What do we now call a Land Rail?

20. What sort of bird is a Johnny Rook?

2017 B
David Lindo – OSME

Answers: page 265

1. What happened to the last pair of Barn Owls that nested in Malta in the last century in 1988?

2. What species was killed while in flight by a fast ball from Jahangir Khan to T. N. Pearce at Lord's Cricket Ground in 1936 and was subsequently stuffed and mounted on the match ball and preserved in the MCC Museum?

3. Name three counties in which Stone-curlew were confirmed to breed in 2014.

4. How do you spell Bagobo Babbler?

5. Do New Zealand Yellowhammers have more dialects than British Yellowhammers (from which they are descended)?

6. In which country has a road been painted with pink, green and yellow strips in an attempt to deter Arctic Terns from nesting thereupon or at least alerting drivers to the presence of the chicks?

7. Why was a gamekeeper, who was filmed shooting a Hen Harrier on a Scottish grouse moor in 2016, not prosecuted?

8. Which of the following birds do not exist: Broad-tailed Nightjar, Square-tailed Nightjar, Long-tailed Nightjar, Slender-tailed Nightjar?

9. In which Eastern Mediterranean country has the President pleaded with his countrymen to stop slaughtering migratory birds and has introduced a hunting season from 15th September to 31st December?

10. What birds may be Tristram's, Hildenbrandt's, Socotra or Spotless?

11. In which island or archipelago might you expect to see Short-eared Owl, Night Heron, King Penguin and Falkland Islands Flightless Steamer Duck?

12. What was the occupation of George Montagu, after whom Montagu's Harrier is named?

13. Which well known artist and huge supporter of conservation and the Birdfair received an MBE in the Queen's Birthday Honours two years ago (2015)?

14. Where would you find the Vampire Ground Finch?

15. According to Jeremy Greenwood, how often should the International Ornithological Congress change its World List, in order to overcome the exasperating confusion caused by perpetual revision (as each new taxonomic opinion is adopted)? Is it every 10 years, every 25 years or every 50 years?

16. What British (and Mexican) bird is Mexico's national bird?

17. What threatens the Critically Endangered Hooded Grebe in its wintering area on the Santa Cruz River?

18. Which bird family has the most species in Category C on the British List – that is, 'introduced but with self-sustaining populations on the British List'?

19. In which year did Birdfair launch the campaign to Save the Albatross which resulted in the setting up of the Albatross Task Force in 2006?

20. What age was the oldest recorded Collared Dove in Britain which was found dead in Orkney in 2015? Was it 18, 19 or 20 years?

2017 C
Tim Jones – BTO

Answers: page 265

1. What happened to the last pair of Jackdaws that nested in Malta in the last century in 1956?

2. Concerning which species did Denis Summers-Smith publish his first article in *British Birds* in 1956 and his most recent in 2016?

3. Which of the following threaten the Critically Endangered Hooded Grebe on its breeding lakes: introduced Rainbow Trout competing for food, Kelp Gulls taking chicks and eggs, introduced American Mink?

4. What was the population of Cirl Buntings in the UK in 2016? Was it approximately 200 pairs, 500 pairs or 1,000 pairs?

5. What bird has its densest population on Bermuda, where it was introduced in 1957 to control the lizards, which were eating the ladybird beetles, which had been introduced to control the cedar scale insects?

6. What species was/is 'Skybomb Bolt'?

7. Which of the following birds do not exist: Pink Robin, Crimson Robin, Rose Robin, Scarlet Robin?

8. Which common Eurasian corvid's south-west Saudi Arabian population has recently been split?

9. How many species does BirdLife recognize, including recently extinct species (on 1st January 2017)? Is it 11,121, 11,221 or 11,321?

10. How many passerine species do they recognize? Is it 5,649, 6,649 or 7,649?

11. What was the occupation of Gilbert White, after whom White's Thrush is named?

12. What birds may be Tiny, Giant, Gorgeous, Beautiful and Souimanga?

13. Do some Icelandic whimbrels migrate to West Africa non-stop?

14. What is the most recent species of gull to be added to the British List?

15. How do you spell Udzungwa Forest-partridge?

16. In which island or archipelago might you expect to see Short-eared Owl, Limpkin, Zapata Sparrow and Gundlach's Hawk?

17. What British bird of prey has Natural England licensed to be killed in order 'to prevent serious damage to young pheasants' (of which 45 million are released every year)?

18. Name one of the two Critically Endangered species in the UK's Overseas Territories.

19. How many occupied Grey Heron nests were there in the UK in 2015? Was it roughly 7,000, 9,000 or 11,000?

20. Which blue-eyed bird was rediscovered in Brazil in 2015 – 75 years after its last documented record?

2017 D
Michael Mills – ABC

Answers: page 266

1. Of the *ringed* birds that are shot in Malta each year, which is the most numerous in terms of ringing recoveries?

2. What species of wild bird was recorded breeding successfully at the bottom of Frickley Colliery, 640 metres below ground, in 1975?

3. How do you spell Chaco Chachalaca?

4. Which large black and white African bird had a European population (mainly in France) of about 5,000 in 2006 following escapes from captivity, requiring culling of 8,000 birds in the following ten years, so that the population is now only a few hundred?

5. Arjan Dwarshuis achieved a World Record Year List in 2016. Was it 4,833, 5,833 or 6,833?

6. What was the last bird he saw at dusk on 31st December 2016?

7. In which year did the BTO commence ringing at Constant Effort Sites? Was it 1963, 1973 or 1983?

8. Which of the following birds do not exist: Scissor-tailed Nightjar, Ladder-tailed Nightjar, Lyre-tailed Nightjar, Fork-tailed Nightjar?

9. What was the name of the 'green' birding team that competed in the 2017 Champions of the Flyway bird race in Israel on bicycles, seeing a very creditable 122 birds (not much less than the Media Birders)?

10. What is the affectionate name by which the female (Chatham) Black Robin, from which all Black Robins are descended, is known?

11. What birds may be Red-faced, Long-tailed, Long-billed, Lemon-bellied or Philippa's?

12. What was the occupation of Thomas Bewick, after whom Bewick's Swan is named?

13. In which English county are Firecrests most abundant?

14. Where do the vast majority of Shelduck go to moult?

15. In which island or archipelago might you expect to see Great Tit, Philippine Megapode, Hose's Broadbill and Mountain Black-eye?

16. In which county in Scotland did a female Crane successfully raise a single young to fledging in 2016, despite losing her partner?

17. Which artist and conservationist painted a famous painting of the Loch Ness Monster in 1975?

18. What colour is the eye of the Critically Endangered Hooded Grebe?

19. In which year, give or take two years, was a Skokholm-ringed Manx Shearwater first recovered off Argentina?

20. How effective has the EU been in preventing the licensing of diclofenac for veterinary use in Spain and other European countries, given its known catastrophic effect on Asian vultures?

SPECIALIST
QUESTIONS

THE BRITISH LIST
Martin Collinson – *British Birds*

Answers: page 266

1. Who is the current Secretary of the BOU Records Committee?

2. How many species are on the British List?

3. What is the first species on the British List?

4. How many editions of *The Checklist* have there been so far?

5. Which species was removed from the British List in January 2003?

6. Which category is Mandarin in?

7. What was the first definition of Category B?

8. What was the name of the taxidermist in the Tadcaster rarities investigation?

9. How many species are in Category B?

10. How many species are in Category C?

11. Which bird, that has subsequently bred, was first recorded in Hampshire on 4th March 1961?

12. What is the most recent addition to the British List?

13. How many species on the British List are formally considered extinct?

14. How many species were deleted from the British List following the rejection of the Hastings Rarities?

15. How many of the species deleted from the British List as Hastings Rarities have subsequently been readmitted to the List on the basis of later records?

16. Who was Chairman of the BOU Records Committee when the sixth edition of *The Checklist* was published in 1992?

17. How many passerines are there in Category B?

18. What is the correct spelling of the scientific name for Stonechat?

19. Which species, recorded on 11th July 1905, has since been removed from the List?

20. Which North American species was added to the British List in December 2001 following a record in November 1999 on the Outer Hebrides?

RSPB
Chris Harbard – *Birdwatch*
Answers: page 266

1. Who was the first President of the Society?

2. From which kinds of birds did the feathers known as 'ospreys' come?

3. What was the Society's 100th reserve?

4. In which year did the Avocet become the logo of the RSPB?

5. In 1961, how much did the Society pay for The Lodge?

6. When did the membership of the RSPB reach a million?

7. Who was Chairman of the Society in 1894?

8. In which year did the RSPB first issue Christmas cards?

9. RSPB Wildlife Explorers was previously called Young Ornithologists' Club (YOC). What was it before that?

10. On which piece of merchandise did the 'Avocet' symbol first appear?

11. In which year was *Bird Notes and News* first published?

12. Who was the RSPB's first employed Scottish representative?

13. What was the first address of the Society?

14. In which year were webcams set up at Loch Garten and South Stack?

15. Which was RSPB's first members' group?

16. What motto appears on the Society's seal?

17. When did the RSPB first sell nest-boxes?

18. The Society's first Watchers were appointed in 1901. What were they to watch?

19. In which year did Ian Prestt become Director?

20. Who was the first Head of the Investigations Unit?

H. G. 'HG' ALEXANDER
Dave Nurney – *Bird Watching*

Answers: page 267

1. Where was HG born?

2. How many brothers did HG have?

3. For what does the 'G' in 'H. G.' stand?

4. To which species of bird, seen and heard on 25th March 1897, did HG attribute his passion for birds?

5. What section did HG contribute to Witherby's *Handbook of British Birds*?

6. Which famous person, and personal friend, did HG first meet in India in 1943?

7. Where was HG educated?

8. In what subject did HG attain a degree at King's College, Cambridge?

9. How old was HG when he was given his first pair of binoculars?

10. With whom did HG write *The Birds of Delhi and District*?

11. What was his first wife's name?

12. To what did HG attribute the interest of himself and his brothers in natural history in general?

13. What species graces the dustcover of *Seventy Years of Birdwatching*?

14. In 1955, which species of *Phylloscopus* did HG correctly predict would be a future vagrant to Britain?

15. What species did HG find nesting in an occupied bed in April 1929?

16. What rarity did he find at Northampton sewage farm on 20th October 1951?

17. To what town did HG move after retiring from Birmingham?

18. In which year was *Seventy Years of Birdwatching* published?

19. What was the subject of HG's first article published in *British Birds*?

20. HG's brother, Wilfrid, was the first Director of which ornithological body?

BARN OWLS
Peter Wilkinson – *BTO News*

Answers: page 267

1. What does *Tyto alba* mean?

2. What is the incubation period of a Barn Owl?

3. Which Italian naturalist first officially described the Barn Owl and so has his name appended to it?

4. In which year did Giovanni Scopoli first describe the Barn Owl?

5. Where does *Tyto alba schmitzi* live?

6. At what wavelength is the Barn Owl's hearing most acute?

7. Which of these is not a subspecies of Barn Owl – *Tyto alba pratincola*, *hibernica*, or *contempta*?

8. In 1932, who did the RSPB sponsor to survey Barn Owls?

9. Barn Owls are probably responsible for the owl hieroglyph in ancient Egyptian script. What sound did this represent?

10. Apart from looking attractive, what does the heart-shaped facial disc help the Barn Owl to do?

11. Which toe is pectinated?

12. What subspecies of Barn Owl breeds in the Galapagos?

13. Which of the following is NOT a local name for the Barn Owl – ullat, cherubim, banshee?

14. Which primary feather is normally the longest in *Tyto alba*?

15. What colour are a Barn Owl's claws?

16. What is the subspecific name of the Dark-breasted Barn Owl?

17. Barn Owls' external ears are asymmetrical. Which ear is higher?

18. In which year was the first currently accepted record of the Dark-breasted Barn Owl in Britain?

19. How long is the fledging period?

20. What do the Californian Indian tribe, the Newuks, believe about the Barn Owl?

BIRDS OF KENYA
David Fisher – Sunbird

Answers: page 267

1. How many endemic species does Kenya have?

2. Which two species, on the Kenya List as vagrants, appear at the top of the African Bird Club web page?

3. Name all the gull species that breed in Kenya.

4. How would you distinguish Great and Long-tailed Cormorant by their eye colour?

5. Which species of American wading bird was recorded for the first time in Kenya in Setember 1999?

6. Name a species parasitised by Steel-blue Whydah.

7. The 'Lightning Bird' appears in more African legends than any other bird, and is generally regarded as an ill omen. What do we know it as?

8. Which rare canopy weaver which occurs in the Kakamega Forest and forages from branches nuthatch-like or tit-like may now be extirpated from Kenya?

9. Name Kenya's two Critically Endangered birds.

10. Which bird's call is sometimes interpreted as the female uttering, 'I'm going, I'm going, I'm going home to my relations', to be answered by the male, 'You can go home, you can go home, you can go home to your relations'?

11. Its scientific name is *Lybius guifsobalito.* What is the common name of this Kenyan species?

12. What species is on the Kenya List on the strength of 'a specimen taken in 1917 at Lake Jipe, but there is no evidence that it was secured in Kenyan territory'?

13. Which Kenyan species has remarkable cat-like pupils that contract to vertical slits, like its American counterpart?

14. How many species of the *Tauraco* genus occur in Kenya?

15. What is the Latin name for Straw-tailed Whydah?

16. How many IBAs (Important Bird Areas) does Kenya have according to BirdLife International?

17. In what pack might you find a Bateleur?

18. Who is the current Bird Recorder for Kenya?

19. Which species is known in Kenya only from specimens taken near Mandera and El Wak in 1901?

20. What is another name for the Mousebird family?

ACCEPTED BRITISH FIRSTS (1983–2005)

Tim Melling – Naturetrek

Answers: page 268

1. What species was originally identified as an Orphean Warbler, when it was first found on Lundy in April 1987?

2. Which species first appeared in Britain in 1987, two years after the first and only other European occurrence in Ireland?

3. Which species was first seen briefly in Cornwall on 22nd June 1988, then 17 days later on 9th July in East Sussex, both single-observer sightings?

4. What was unusual about the Spectacled Warbler trapped at Filey in May 1992 when released?

5. Where was Britain's first Wilson's Warbler found?

6. Name two species first recorded in 1989 that were also seen in 1990.

7. How many people were estimated to have seen the Golden-winged Warbler on the first weekend of its stay at Tescos in Larkfield, Kent, in 1989?

8. Which first remained a single-observer sighting as the only person the finder was able to contact refused to leave his Sunday dinner (by the time he arrived, the bird had gone, never to be seen again)?

9. Which first for Britain was found on the same date as the first Short-billed Dowitcher for Ireland?

10. Mark Chapman found the Brown Shrike on 30th September 1985 at Sumburgh, Shetland. Why was this a coincidence for Mark?

11. How many tail feathers did the Mourning Dove have on the Calf of Man in 1989 and why was this significant in its identification?

12. At which east coast site were two species added to the British List less than five years apart in autumn 1981 and summer 1986?

13. What were the birds?

14. Which species was added to the British List largely on the basis of a supporting video recording taken near Land's End in 1995?

15. When was the Cedar Waxwing seen in Shetland in 1985 finally upgraded to Category A on the British List?

16. How many days did the Double-crested Cormorant that was sighted at Billingham, Cleveland, in 1989, stay?

17. Which current member of RSPB staff found a short-staying British first at Portland Bill in 1992 while leading a YOC group?

18. How many firsts in this period have been recorded in Dorset?

19. What first was seen on Fair Isle in May 1985, and the first for Norway was seen on the 29th September 1985, but it remains in Category D?

20. The wild origins of the Anglesey Grey Catbird in October 2001 were supported by the arrival of which Nearctic passerine in Anglesey on the same day?

BIRDS OF HAMPSHIRE
Nigel Jones – Ornitholidays

Answers: page 268

1. In which year was Little Ringed Plover first proved to breed in Hampshire?

2. Which rare summer migrant was recorded breeding for the first time in Hampshire in 1897, raising three young at Mottisfont?

3. Which author of a Hampshire avifauna was also a long-serving member of the RSPB Council?

4. When was Edwin Cohen's *Birds of Hampshire and the Isle of Wight* first published?

5. Which former breeding species was last recorded in Hampshire on 12th January 1910?

6. Which bird was first proved breeding in Britain in the New Forest in 1962?

7. Which songbird had its first British record in Hampshire when it was shot by the Earl of Malmesbury (in 1828 near Christchurch)?

8. White Rump, Horse-match and Horse-musher are local Hampshire names for which species which used to be shot for the pot?

9. Which two species appeared on the dust jacket of *Birds of Hampshire*, the county avifauna, edited by Clarke & Eyre, 1993?

10. A bird of which species was found dead at Milford on Sea on 19 November 1911 and represents the only English record?

11. Which rare songbird had its only Hampshire record rejected in a recent review by the British Birds Rarities Committee (two birds at Totton on 13th August 1951)?

12. Which species of gamebird was introduced into the New Forest by the Hon. Gerald Lascelles in the 1880s, although they failed to establish themselves?

13. When was the first Collared Dove recorded in Hampshire?

14. In what year was Cetti's Warbler first recorded in Hampshire (and Britain)?

15. What was it misidentified as?

16. As what do we know Gilbert White's 'Large shivering willow-wren' nowadays?

17. Which songbird had its first British record in Hampshire in 1852, then no further county records for more than 100 years?

18. Which former breeding species was last recorded in Hampshire on 26th October 1936?

19. Little Egret is now a Hampshire breeding bird, but when was the first ever Hampshire record?

20. For which species is Southsea Castle the premier Hampshire locality?

LARGE GULLS OF THE NORTHERN HEMISPHERE
Brian Small – Limosa

Answers: page 268

1. How many subspecies of *Larus cachinnans* were listed in Howard and Moore's checklist of birds of the world?

2. Which species of large gull is on the British List by virtue of a single individual dating from 1859 in Devon?

3. Where are the nearest breeding Glaucous Gulls to the UK?

4. What is the average clutch size of the Great Black-backed Gull in the UK?

5. In which year did BOU Records Committee announce the acceptance of the taxon *cachinnans* onto the British List?

6. Where in Spain do Great Black-backed Gulls breed?

7. What is 'Nelson's' Gull?

8. How many races are there of Great Black-backed Gull?

9. When or where was the first British record of *michahellis*?

10. Witherby examined the specimen of the first British record of *michahellis* and famously misidentified it in *The Handbook of British Birds*. As what form did Witherby misidentify the specimen?

11. What non-hormonal chemical pollutant causes feminisation of the embryo of the Western Gull, resulting in a skewed sex ratio?

12. Where, until about 50 years ago, did nearly all Lesser Black-backed Gulls winter?

13. What nationality was Heuglin, after whom Heuglin's Gull is named?

14. Specifically speaking, what do Caspian Gull and Black-headed Gull have in common?

15. When and where was the first reported successful breeding of non-hybrid pairs of *michahellis* in Britain?

16. Which species did Dwight suggest the voice of *cachinnans* resembled in his treatise?

17. When was the taxon *cachinnans* first described?

18. Which species of gull is the most numerous urban roof-nester in the UK?

19. Who was the famous Dutchman who worked in England on instinctive behaviour in large gulls and wrote *The Study of Instinct*?

20. In which region of Europe have Yellow-legged Gulls been culled in the past as a species protection measure?

THE HISTORY OF BIRDWATCHING IN BRITAIN
Stephen Moss – Leica

Answers: page 269

1. What famous birder's portrait has followed the fortunes of the RSPB?

2. Which Foreign Secretary wrote a classic book on birdwatching?

3. In which year was the Edward Grey Institute of Field Ornithology founded?

4. What was the original title of the magazine *Birding World*, first produced in 1987?

5. Titchwell's Black-winged Stilt was Sam and Shetland's Black-browed Albatross was Albert. But who was Elsie?

6. Who was the first Secretary of the BTO, in whose name an annual medal is awarded for services to ornithology?

7. Who was the first President of Shetland Bird Club, discovered Fetlar's breeding Snowy Owls and attempted to photograph them dressed as a pantomime horse?

8. Which species of British breeding bird was the first to have their nests protected?

9. Almost 100 years ago, on what date was the first *British Birds* published?

10. Who was first Warden of Dungeness?

11. In what year was the pager introduced?

12. The mammoth work, *Birds of the Western Palaearctic* was a collaborative effort. How many editors were involved in the last volume?

13. Which MP presented a history of the RSPB on Radio 4 in June this year?

14. Who wrote the text for Volume I (Land Birds) of *A History of British Birds* by Thomas Bewick?

15. In August 1962 *British Birds* devoted an entire issue to investigating a controversy, the conclusions of which were described as 'painful and shocking'. What was the subject?

16. How many species were removed from the British List after the 'Hastings Rarities' affair?

17. When was the Royal Charter given to the RSPB?

18. Which of the trio of Alexander brothers opened up the field of marine ornithology with his 1928 book *Birds of the Ocean*?

19. In 1996 the group with the acronym ACRE was set up. What does the acronym stand for?

20. Which 7th-century hermit has been described as Britain's first bird conservationist?

ENDEMIC BIRDS OF ETHIOPIA
Chris Galvin – Swarovski

Answers: page 269

1. What Ethiopian endemic did Rüppell discover around Shoa?

2. There are 29 species endemic to Ethiopia AND ERITREA. How many are endemic to Ethiopia alone?

3. The Italian ornithologist Salvadori named a turaco after its discoverer, Prince Ruspoli. In which year is the discovery thought to have been made – 1892, 1911 or 1913?

4. What caused Prince Ruspoli's death in the year following his ornithological discovery?

5. Of where was Prince Ruspoli the Prince?

6. The specific name of the Spot-breasted Plover does not refer to the spotty breast but to what feature?

7. Which species is portrayed on the 35 cent stamp in the Endemic Birds of Ethiopia stamp series issued in 1989?

8. Which endemic is known only from a wing found as a road-kill?

9. Which wing was it?

10. Name one of the two endemic species that Bill Oddie identified from the window of the gents' toilet at Addis Ababa airport before being escorted out at gunpoint?

11. The English names of two Ethiopian endemics commemorate German ornithologists, but only one describes the bird named after him. Which?

12. Who described Stresemann's Bush-crow in honour of the other famous German ornithologist?

13. Why is the White-winged Swallow a mega bird?

14. What threatens Prince Ruspoli's Turaco besides habitat loss?

15. Although discovered in 1942, no White-tailed Swallow's nest was found until 1996. Was it a) in a termite mound, b) in a well-shaft or c) in a native-hut?

16. Rüppell discovered an Ethiopian endemic during an ambush on the Takazee River in 1832. What was it?

17. The second recorded specimen of which species was presented to Major R. E. Cheesman in 1927 by the inhabitants of Bichena, who regarded it as the finest table bird?

18. Erlanger's Lark, regarded as either an endemic species or an endemic race of Red-capped Lark, was named after Carlo Freiherr von Erlanger, who died in 1904. What was noteworthy about his death?

19. Whose name is commemorated in the generic, specific and common name of an Ethiopian endemic?

20. What is the largest endemic Ethiopian passerine?

BRITISH BIRDS RARITIES COMMITTEE AND BRITISH RARITIES IN THE 1990s

Colin Bradshaw – Carl Zeiss

Answers: page 269

1. At which British mainland site did two American sparrow species occur in consecutive years in the 1990s?

2. In which county did both Collared and Black-winged Pratincoles occur in 1997?

3. The submission of which rare bird in 1995 contained the description 'like an Oystercatcher on steroids'?

4. In which year did Albert the Black-browed Albatross last appear at a Shetland Gannet colony?

5. Which Asiatic thrush delighted East London birders at Woodford Green in early 1990?

6. Which wader species, discovered just before the 1997 Birdfair, was initially misidentified as its marginally less rare relative?

7. The 125 records of this species in 1992 showed no imbalance between the sexes, whereas the 19 in 1994 showed a preponderance of females. What was the species?

8. In early 1996 which inland county played host to two potential firsts for Britain (one of which later proved to be the second record)?

9. Where did the second British Redhead occur (in 1997)?

10. Which acceptance process of which new species to Britain included the identification of Red Fescue and Ribwort Plantain?

11. Which rarity in 1994 was seen at 7.30 a.m. in West Yorkshire and at midday in Cumbria?

12. Which British rarity was recorded only 14 times up to 1999, but was then recorded 12 times in 1999?

13. Which common American dove was finally added to the British List following a record in the Outer Hebrides in November 1999?

14. Which warbler species, recorded in 1992, was a first for Britain despite no fewer than three prior records having been accepted but later rejected?

15. In 1995, which site joined the tiny club which have had both Ross's and Ivory Gulls?

16. What was the accepted age and sex of Norfolk's Red-breasted Nuthatch?

17. Which American wood warbler has occurred four times in Britain, all on Scottish islands, the last of which was in 1995?

18. At what location was the first British female Lesser Scaup recorded in 1996?

19. Which eastern wader, the third British record, frequented a horse paddock in Norfolk in May 1993?

20. In what year was the female Swinhoe's Storm-petrel first tape-lured at Tynemouth?

BIRDS OF BRITAIN
Adrian Thomas – WildSounds

Answers: page 270

1. Name two species on the British List named after countries.

2. Which IUCN Red Data species is currently being reintroduced near Peterborough?

3. When was the last year that Ospreys were recorded nesting in Britain before the recent recolonisation?

4. Which rare bird in the UK was thought to have been seen by the greatest number of people?

5. What is the most recent species to have been admitted to the British List?

6. Who successfully introduced the Little Owl into Britain?

7. Who first unsuccessfully introduced the Little Owl into Britain?

8. Which winter visitor is known in Scotland as 'Coal-and-candle-light'?

9. Which species appears first on the newly organised BOU list of British birds?

10. In what year was Collared Dove first recorded in Britain?

11. What is the former name for Common Rosefinch?

12. Which British bird has 44 recognised subspecies spread across four continents?

13. 1863 and 1888 were the two largest recent irruptions to Britain of which species?

14. Which passerine was added to the British List when seen briefly at Cley by the two leading lights of Birdline on 14th June 1981?

15. Britain has three breeding species on the IUCN Red Data list that are Near Threatened and one that is Data Deficient. What is the Data Deficient species?

16. Which species was recorded from the most 10 km squares in the original 1968–72 Atlas survey?

17. Which British bird derives its Linnaean name from a word meaning 'money changer'?

18. Who first described Roseate Tern?

19. How many species of tit in the family Paridae occur in Britain?

20. What is the redcap in John Clare's poem, which begins: 'The redcap is a painted bird/And beautiful its feathers are./In early spring its voice is heard/Searching thistles brown and bare'?

ALBATROSSES
Chris Harbard – OSME

Answers: page 270

1. How many species of albatross does BirdLife International consider to be Globally Threatened with extinction?

2. Which famous American ornithologist wrote (on 28th October 1912): 'I now belong to a higher cult of mortals for I have seen the albatross'?

3. What most obviously distinguishes Campbell Albatross from Black-browed?

4. What is the minimum wind speed required for an albatross to remain airborne?

5. Apart from Pyramid, on what other island has the Chatham Albatross attempted to breed at least once?

6. The Waved Albatross was considered to be globally Vulnerable until the 2007 Red List changed this classification to what level of threat?

7. What species of albatross is known variously as Pio, Piew, Pee-arr, Peole, Blue bird and Stinkpot?

8. For what species was a light railway constructed on the island of Torishima to carry the corpses of slaughtered birds from the breeding slopes to the beach for the feather trade in the 19th century?

9. How many Black-footed Albatrosses are thought to be killed every year due to long-line fishing, according to BirdLife International?

10. What was the local name of the Short-tailed Albatross in Alaska?

11. Off what country are the majority of Chatham Albatrosses now thought to winter?

12. How did the Ancient Mariner in Coleridge's *The Rime of the Ancient Mariner* kill the albatross?

13. What is the nearest to the UK that Short-tailed Albatross is known to have bred?

14. What is the population of mature adults of the Critically Endangered Amsterdam Albatross, to the nearest 10?

15. Name another country where Laysan Albatross breeds apart from the USA (Hawaii)

16. Which bird uses stones to break the eggs of Black-footed and Laysan Albatrosses on the Hawaiian archipelago?

17. Name one of the three islands in the Falkland Islands containing colonies of over 50,000 pairs of Black-browed Albatross.

18. How is smoking a danger to albatrosses?

19. Apart from Tristan Albatross, which species of albatross breed on the Tristan archipelago?

20. How many forms (species) of Great Albatross are there?

BIRDS OF CAMEROON
Mark Andrews – ABC

Answers: page 271

1. How many species are endemic solely to Mount Cameroon?

2. What are they?

3. What is the alternative name for the Green-winged Pytilia?

4. In which other country is the Cameroon Sunbird found?

5. On what date in 2006 was Cameroon's first Verreaux's Eagle recorded?

6. What two species of weaver found in Cameroon are considered Threatened?

7. How many kingfishers are on the Cameroon list?

8. What race of Pink-footed Puffback is resident in Cameroon?

9. What colour is the iris of the Adamawa Turtle Dove?

10. What is the average clutch size of the Grey-necked Picathartes?

11. What is the Threatened category of the Grey-necked Picathartes?

12. What is the only tropicbird on the Cameroon list?

13. Who described Bates's Weaver *Ploceus batesi*, the specimens of which were shot by boys with bows and arrows and were never actually seen alive by George Latimer Bates?

14. What Cameroon bird lays the smallest egg in relation to its size?

15. Who was the Ursula that the near-endemic sunbird was named after?

16. What is the only crane to occur in Cameroon?

17. Who was responsible for the discovery of a disjunct population of the Bamenda Apalis on the Adamawa Plateau in 1974?

18. Where else in Africa does the White-naped Pigeon occur apart from Cameroon?

19. What is the scientific name for Freckled Nightjar?

20. According to the African Bird Club systematic list of Cameroon, what is the final bird on the Cameroon list?

THE ENDEMIC SPECIES AND SUBSPECIES OF TAIWAN
Paul French – OBC

Answers: page 271

1. Is the local race of Black-chinned Fruit-dove larger or smaller than the nominate race?

2. In which year did Gould write his paper on 16 new species from Taiwan?

3. What bird has a local name of King of the Mist?

4. What is the alternative name for the Taiwan Magpie?

5. Which endemic species breeds co-operatively?

6. What is the main threat to the Taiwan Hwamei?

7. Swinhoe's Pheasant *Lophura swinhoii* was originally placed in what genus by John Gould in 1863 before it was subsequently placed in *Lophura*?

8. Which bird became known as National Day Bird?

9. Why were hundreds of thousands of Grey-faced Buzzards killed prior to the 1980s when it became the National Day Bird?

10. What colour is the rump of the Taiwanese race of Common Pheasant?

11. Which bird did Robert Swinhoe suggest for use on the armorial bearings of Taiwan, should it ever become a European colony?

12. What was the problem with the first male specimen of the Whistling Green Pigeon that Swinhoe acquired in Taiwan in 1865?

13. How many endemic subspecies of babbler found only on Taiwan did Dr Carpenter consider could be regarded as distinct species in his study reported in 2006?

14. What is the scientific subspecies name of White-browed Shortwing that is found in Taiwan?

15. What is the typical habitat of the White-eared Sibia?

16. Which Taiwanese endemic is somehow linked with a species of panda?

17. What was the occupation of Frederick Styan (of Bulbul and Panda fame)?

18. What is the chief threat to Styan's Bulbul?

19. The Latin name for Taiwan Partridge is *Arborophila crudigularis*. What does *crudigularis* mean?

20. Which of Mikado and Swinhoe's Pheasants was described first?

ENDEMIC BIRDS OF COLOMBIA
Carl Downing – NBC

Answers: page 272

1. In which type of habitat does the Endangered Sapphire-bellied Hummingbird occur?

2. Which celebrated bird artist is commemorated in the name of a Colombian endemic bird?

3. How many endemics are named after the Santa Marta Mountains?

4. What is *Penelope perspicax*?

5. What do Apolinar's Wren and Niceforo's Wren have in common (other than the obvious)?

6. Which subspecies of Blossomcrown is found in the Central Andes in Tolima and Huila?

7. The Rusty-headed Spinetail is endemic to which mountain range in Columbia?

8. What is the only member of the Colombidae family that is endemic to Colombia?

9. Who was the Albert commemorated in the Latin name of the Blue-billed Curassow *Crax alberti*?

10. Who recently discovered the Gorgeted Puffleg?

11. Which former Colombian endemic, which defied even Ted Parker to identify it, has recently been discovered in Ecuador?

12. Surprisingly, the great collector of Colombian birds, Melbourne Armstrong Carriker, has his name commemorated in the name of just one subspecies of Colombian endemic bird. Which?

13. How many races of White-mantled Barbet are there?

14. What is the scientific name of the Rufous-fronted Parakeet?

15. 'Corcovado Gorgiblanco' is the Spanish name for which Colombian endemic?

16. How many species of hummingbird are endemic to Colombia?

17. How many species of Colombian endemics are currently ranked as Globally Threatened (Vulnerable or above), to the nearest five?

18. How many eggs does the Multicoloured Tanager lay?

19. At the last count, how many endemic species of tapaculo of the genus *Scytalopus* does Colombia possess?

20. Name a Starfrontlet species endemic to Colombia?

CRITICALLY ENDANGERED BIRDS OF THE NEOTROPICS
Martin Fowlie – NBC

Answers: page 272

1. Is the Black Curassow one of the Critically Endangered Cracidae species?

2. The Short-crested Coquette is endemic to which country?

3. Royal Cinclodes was only classified as Critically Endangered after being split from which species of Least Concern?

4. Which of the Critically Endangered Darwin's finches is restricted to Isabela Island?

5. Which Critically Endangered hummingbird species is almost entirely confined to Volcan Pinchincha in Ecuador?

6. The last remaining wild male Spix's Macaw paired with a female of which different species?

7. Which Colombian species has been greatly helped by the use of nest-boxes?

8. One of the world's most sexually dimorphic hummingbirds is found on which Chilean island?

9. What other Critically Endangered species occurs on the Juan Fernandez Islands?

10. Name one Critically Endangered species endemic to Hispaniola.

11. How many Critically Endangered macaws are there in the Neotropics?

12. Which Critically Endangered species has not been seen for 185 years?

13. How many Critically Endangered species are listed for Argentina?

14. Munchique National Park in Brazil is one of only two locations where the Munchique Wood-wren is found. What is the other?

15. What parasite threatens the Pale-headed Brush-finch in Ecuador with an overall 42% parasitism rate?

16. Who was Lear of Lear's Macaw?

17. Which neotropical country holds the distinction of hosting the highest number of Critically Endangered species?

18. Which is the only Critically Endangered Ground Dove of the genus *Columbina* in the neotropical region?

19. The Royal Cinclodes of the southern Peruvian and northern Bolivian Andes is restricted to which type of high-elevation, endangered forest?

20. Why is the Polylepis forest, where the Royal Cinclodes occurs, particularly threatened?

THE BIRDS OF THE SCILLY ISLES, 1997–2007
Paul Stancliffe – BTO

Answers: page 273

1. Who broke the record for number of species seen in one year in 2002 (with 229–31)?

2. What species, which has occurred every year from 1997 to 2007, took 23 years to identify?

3. How many swift species were seen in the Scilly Isles during 2002?

4. What is the connection between the first records of Marsh Sandpiper and Ovenbird

5. Which first for Scilly, present on Bryher from 24th to 28th September 2001, was retrospectively identified from photographs?

6. Why was 16th May 2002 a bad day to play golf?

7. In which winter did a Whimbrel winter in the Scillies?

8. What species of raptor bred in Scilly for the first time in 2005?

9. Which common migrant had its largest ever fall on 15th October 1999?

10. How long did the 2001 Chough stay?

11. How many firsts for Britain appeared in the Scillies in 1999?

12. The April 2000 Collared Pratincole was found on St Mary's and was also seen on St Martin's. What other island did it visit?

13. With what large object is the 2003 Scilly Little Swift depicted in the November 2004 edition of *British Birds*?

14. On 22 March 2002 a report was received of 'a black and white bird' on Wingletang. What did it turn out to be?

15. Which species was only seen in the Scilly Isles for the second time on 2 August 2002?

16. Dusky Warbler has been recorded eight times between 1997 and 2006 on all but one of the five main islands. Which one?

17. Which species was found on 14 October 2003 and was only the second record for the Scillies?

18. How many Serins were seen or heard in the Scilly Isles in 1998?

19. Prior to the 2001 record of Magpie on St Martin's, how many Magpies had previously been recorded on Scilly?

20. What species was shown on the cover of the *Isles of Scilly Bird and Natural History Review* for 2002?

THE BIRDS OF SYRIA
David Murdoch – OSME

Answers: page 273

1. Who rediscovered the Northern Bald Ibis in Syria in 2002?

2. Apart from Northern Bald Ibis, what other species classified as Critically Endangered occurs in Syria?

3. The basalt desert of southern Syria is home to a black-headed morph whose nominate form is white headed. What is the species?

4. What was this bird formerly thought to be?

5. When did the Ostrich become extinct in Syria?

6. The first and second records of Pine Bunting in Syria came from the same place. Where was it?

7. How many species of Globally Threatened birds occur in Syria?

8. All records of Palestine Sunbird in Syria come from one season. Which season?

9. How many Important Bird Areas have been identified in Syria?

10. What bird links Knutsford, Cheshire, with Damascus?

11. At least eight individuals of which Vulnerable species were recently observed at Buhayrat al-Basil in February 2007?

12. In 1879 two of which species of owl were collected at the Kabir River in northern Syria?

13. Which zoologist wrote about Syrian birds in the 1930s and 1940s, but is probably most famous for finding the wild Golden Hamster (and her litter) in 1930, which is the ancestor of all pet hamsters?

14. How many Threatened passerines are there in Syria?

15. What is it?

16. Name one of the two *(three)* Near Threatened passerines.

17. Which sawbill, previously considered a vagrant to Syria, was recently discovered to be quite numerous in Buhayrat al-Basil when 15 birds were seen?

18. How many Slavonian Grebes have been recorded from Syria?

19. Name a Syrian wheatear named after a person?

20. The largest rail in the Western Palearctic breeds in northwest Syria. What is it?

THE BIRDS OF ZAMBIA
Pete Leonard – ABC

Answers: page 273

1. How many endemic species does Zambia have?

2. What is the only part of Zambia where the Blue Swallow breeds?

3. Only two BTO-ringed birds have been recovered in Zambia. Name one.

4. How many species of Globally Threatened bird occur in Zambia?

5. Which of the 12 Threatened species is classified as Endangered?

6. Where is the stronghold of the Shoebill in Zambia?

7. There are two races of Tinkling Cisticola *Cisticola rufilatus* in Zambia. What are they?

8. Where are they located?

9. How much does it cost for an overseas subscription to the Zambian Ornithological Society?

10. Which family of birds featured on a set of Zambian stamps issued on 1st June 1998?

11. What was surprising about the parrots depicted on the June 1998 stamps?

12. Which of the 13 species of kingfisher recorded in Zambia was the most recent to be added to the list?

13. What bird links Mrs Gabriel Ellison MBE with the Zambian people's ability to rise above the nation's problems?

14. How many bird species have been recorded in Zambia?

15. Who compiled the checklist for the Zambian Ornithological Society in 2002?

16. Where was the first record for Zambia of Western Reef Heron found?

17. What colour is the iris of Chaplin's Barbet?

18. Which is the only one of Zambia's eight nightjars not to belong to the genus *Caprimulgus*?

19. What species found in Zambia has the Latin name *Ephippiorhynchus senegalensis*?

20. Who wrote the foreword to *Birds of Zambia* published in 1971?

BIRDS OF ETHIOPIA AND THE HORN OF AFRICA
Nigel Redman – ABC

Answers: page 274

1. Which Endangered *Acrocephalus* warbler can be found in the region?

2. Which bird might be assumed to be endemic to Socotra, but is not?

3. Which two rivers are particularly important in shaping the avian geography of south-east Ethiopia and southern Somalia?

4. With what other species does Ethiopian Bush-crow often associate?

5. How many Critically Endangered species have been recorded in Somalia?

6. What species from the region appeared on the Birdfair programme cover in 2007?

7. Name one primarily North African/Middle Eastern species that is known to breed in Djibouti but nowhere else in the region?

8. Name the two Near Threatened species of duck that occur in the Horn of Africa.

9. Who published the recent paper proposing the split of Abd al kuri Sparrow and Socotra Sparrow from Rufous Sparrow?

10. Which species of Robin-chat is recorded at the highest elevation in the Horn of Africa?

11. Which falcon apparently migrates in large numbers through Somalia in spring but has only recently been confirmed to occur in Ethiopia?

12. Name two Globally Threatened serins that are found in Ethiopia.

13. Which British ornithologist described the Somali endemic, the Lesser Hoopoe-lark?

14. How many Globally Threatened birds occur in Ethiopia?

15. Which species was named for the wife of Sir Geoffrey Archer, political administrator of British Somaliland at the start of the 20th century?

16. Which Ethiopian endemic was, until three months ago, known only from a wing found as a road-kill?

17. Which wing was it?

18. Two species of Golden-winged Grosbeak are now recognised in the region. Their scientific names are *socotranus* and *louisae*. Who was Louise?

19. What is the closest relative of the Southern African taxon Carp's Tit that occurs in the Horn of Africa?

20. How many Globally Threatened species have been recorded in Eritrea?

THE BIRDS OF LEBANON
Richard Prior – OSME

Answers: page 274

1. What is the only Endangered species to occur in Lebanon?

2. Which Near Threatened species of shearwater has been recorded in Lebanon?

3. What is the only species in the family Nectariniidae to occur in Lebanon?

4. Which flightless bird no longer occurs in Lebanon?

5. In which year was *Birds of Lebanon* published by ICBP?

6. The author of *Birds of Lebanon* was S. Vere Benson. For what does the initial 'S' stand?

7. Which relative of an emperor described the Syrian Serin?

8. How many Globally Threatened species are native resident, migrant or passage species in Lebanon?

9. Of the six *(eleven)* species of Globally Threatened bird that have been recorded in Lebanon, name the two non-raptors.

10. Which Lebanese bird is named after Henry James Bruce, an American missionary?

11. What is the largest species of pipit that occurs in Lebanon?

12. In what year was the Society for the Protection of Nature in Lebanon, the BirdLife partner, founded?

13. How many species of bunting have been recorded in Lebanon? Is it 5, 8 or 10 *(11)*?

14. In what year did Ramadan-Jaradi & Ramadan-Jaradi first publish their list of the *Birds of Lebanon*?

15. Where is the only specimen of Brown Fish-owl collected in Lebanon held, according to Benson?

16. In his 1997 paper in *Sandgrouse*, Dr Ramadan-Jaradi reported on a number of new breeding species for Lebanon. Name two of the three that were introductions.

17. How many Important Bird Areas does BirdLife list for Lebanon?

18. Name two Important Bird Areas in Lebanon where Syrian Serin has been recorded?

19. How many species of *Prunella* have been recorded in Lebanon?

20. What member of the genus Tarsiger has been recorded in Lebanon?

THREATENED BIRDS OF ASIA
Jez Bird – OBC

Answers: page 275

1. Which is the only species of malkoha that is considered Threatened?

2. What does Black Shama have in common with this year's Birdfair symbol?

3. What year was the Pink-headed Duck last conclusively seen in the wild?

4. What is the total estimated range (in square kilometres) of the Cebu Flowerpecker, which is known only from the island of Cebu in the Philippines.

5. Name two of the five species of Asian bustard that are considered threatened.

6. In which country was the last confirmed record of Slender-billed Curlew in April 2001, according to BirdLife International?

7. What superpower does *Habroptila wallacii* of Halmahera possess?

8. One of the many threats to the Forest Owlet is hunting. What bizarre use is made of some of the body parts?

9. Which is the only Asian swift to appear on the Red List?

10. In what year was the last *confirmed* sighting of Crested Shelduck?

11. In which locality was the last confirmed sighting of Crested Shelduck?

12. Name the species of white-eye that is endemic to the island of Buru in Indonesia.

13. Which Endangered nocturnal species is named after a former British soldier who fought in the Crimean War?

14. Which famous ornithologist described Elliot's Pheasant?

15. Which two Asian woodcock species are on the Red List?

16. Name one of the three islands where the Visayan Wattled Broadbill occurs in the Philippines.

17. Name one of the two islands where the Visayan Wrinkled Hornbill (Rufous-headed Hornbill) occurs in the Philippines.

18. Name a Critically Endangered species restricted to the Indonesian island of Sangihe.

19. Name two of the seven species of Asian pitta that are considered Globally Threatened.

20. Give the dates, a decade apart, of the first collected specimens and the last confirmed sighting of the White-eyed River Martin.

EXTINCT BIRDS SINCE 1600
Martin Fowlie – NBC

Answers: page 275

1. Name the extinct cousin of the Dodo.

2. What was the name of the last Passenger Pigeon?

3. When did Martha die?

4. In which zoo did Martha, the last Passenger Pigeon, and Incas, the last Carolina Parakeet, who died in 1918, both die?

5. Which famous explorer and naturalist was the first (and last) to encounter the Spectacled or Pallas's Cormorant?

6. Which Pacific island species was eaten to extinction by Japanese soldiers during World War II?

7. To what genus do Bourne et al propose moving the Ascension Crake *Atlantisia elpenor* in their 2003 publication?

8. What did the only extinct coua purportedly eat?

9. Which extinct pigeon apparently fed on freshwater molluscs *and fruit*?

10. Where, in 1775, was the last set of Dodo bones destroyed by fire because they were thought to be too shoddy to display?

11. Which species included in some lists of extinct birds was recently deemed a 'banquet of codswallop' in a paper by Storrs Olson?

12. What was the common name of *Ciridops anna*?

13. Which extinct pigeon has the same name as a Premiership soccer team?

14. Which species is the Réunion Solitaire now considered to have been?

15. What is the only species in the family Icteridae that has become extinct?

16. Why was Pallas's Cormorant though to have become extinct?

17. Which year was the last Great Auk seen alive, according to BirdLife?

18. What mammal is included in the name of the extinct emu – *Dromaius baudinianus*?

19. How many species of O'o in the genus *Moho* have become extinct?

20. Which famous North American ornithologist, whose name lives on in a shearwater, described the extinct Grand Cayman Thrush?

BIRDS OF MADAGASCAR
Pete Morris – ABC

Answers: page 275

1. What Malagasy bird family, comprising up to four species, became extinct in the 17th century?

2. Until recently, what was Nuthatch Vanga known as?

3. What colour are the eyes of the Madagascar White (Sacred) Ibis?

4. Which Madagascar endemic was rather surprisingly reported from Tanzania recently?

5. Following the declaration of the Alaotra Grebe as extinct, how many Critically Endangered species are there in Madagascar?

6. Which Endangered raptor has a scientific name that loosely translates as 'hawk with three fine testicles'?

7. Which bird species is depicted on the cover of Sinclair and Langrand's 1998 guide to birds of the Indian Ocean Islands?

8. According to BirdLife International, to what regionally endemic bird family does Crossley's Babbler belong?

9. Which species was first seen in 1931 but not again for 58 years?

10. To what sort of animal had the generic name *Mesites* already been given, thereby necessitating the name *Mesitornis* for mesites?

11. What is the clutch size of the Brown Mesite?

12. Which wader was not only a first for Madagascar in 2002 but also a first for Africa?

13. In 2010 the Alaotra Grebe was declared Extinct. In which decade was the most recent endemic bird extinction on Madagascar prior to this date?

14. What was the most recent Asity (Philepittidae) to be described in 1933, although ten specimens had been collected in the 19th century?

15. What unorthodox examination will Constantine Benson probably have performed on the specimen of Benson's Rock Thrush, which he collected in 1938?

16. Madagascar's greenbuls (tetrakas) are no longer considered to be bulbuls. But what are they?

17. According to BirdLife International, how many extant bird families are there endemic to the island of Madagascar?

18. Is the Madagascar Cuckoo-roller larger than the Comoro Cuckoo-roller?

19. Which subspecies of Madagascar Pygmy Kingfisher is known from only one record in 1974?

20. What was the volume of the egg of the Madagascar Elephant bird *Aepyornis maximus*?

BORNEAN ENDEMICS
James Eaton – OBC

Answers: page 276

1. Name the only Bornean endemic which is classified as Endangered by BirdLife International.

2. The stunning endemic Blue-headed Pitta was formerly placed in a monotypic genus on the basis of dark purplish-blue underparts, unique among pittas. What was the name of this genus?

3. Apart from the Bornean or Black Oriole *Oriolus hosii*, what other Bornean endemic commemorates Charles Hose in its scientific name?

4. Which endemic is named after Mrs Hose?

5. Which endemic graces the back cover of Phillipps's *Field Guide to the Birds of Borneo*?

6. What is the scientific name of the only endemic bird family in Borneo?

7. Which plumage feature distinguishes male Bristleheads from females?

8. Which species has proved to be more common than first thought as it is not hunted since it is considered to be inedible?

9. Which Bornean endemic is the result of a 'dodgy' split?

10. How does the head of the adult Bornean Laughing-thrush differ from the head of the immature?

11. Name one of the two endemics which have a mutualistic relationship with bearded pigs?

12. Which endemic raptor is only found in Sabah?

13. In *The Field Book of a Jungle Wallah*, Charles Hose writes that only one egg of the Bristlebird had ever been found, which was in the Sarawak Museum in Kuching. What was unusual about its discovery?

14. Apart from the Kinabalu Serpent-eagle *Spilornis kinabaluensis*, which other endemic has *kinabaluensis* as its specific name?

15. Which endemic pitta is an inhabitant of upland forest?

16. Which is the smallest of the three endemic barbets?

17. Apart from Blue-banded and Blue-headed Pitta, what is the third endemic pitta?

18. Where in 1985 was the first Bulwer's Pheasant nest discovered?

19. Which of the Bornean endemics was described by Sharpe in 1892?

20. Why is the generic name of Bornean Peacock-pheasant *Polyplectron*?

BRITISH BIRD RARITIES IN THE 1980s

Stuart Elsom – NBC

Answers: page 276

1. Although now a regularly occurring rarity, Lesser Scaup was first recorded at Chasewater, Staffordshire on 8th March 1987. How many more had been discovered in Britain by the end of that decade?

2. In 1984 a Trumpeter Finch was present at Church Norton, West Sussex, from 19th to 23rd May, but what got to the bird before some of the slower twitchers?

3. Name one of the two Palaearctic firsts for Britain on Scilly in 1987.

4. Name one of the two Nearctic firsts for Britain on Scilly in 1987.

5. The second record of Northern Mockingbird was a suppressed bird on Horsey Island, Essex, between 17th and 23rd May 1988. What animal did the landowner cite as his reason for not allowing access to Horsey Island to more than just a select few?

6. In which year were ten species removed from the list of British Birds Rarities?

7. One of those ten species was later reinstated as a British Birds rarity. Which one?

8. On 10th January 1981 an unattached leg, bearing a ring, was found at Fishburn, County Durham. What rarity had it earlier been attached to?

9. How many different individual Swinhoe's Petrels were trapped at Tynemouth during the 1980s?

10. The 1982 Varied Thrush in Cornwall lacked orange in its plumage. What is the scientific name for this condition?

11. Which now near-annual rarity was recorded only three times in the 1980s, once in Lincolnshire at Theddlethorpe Dunes and twice on Shetland?

12. In July 1981 two UK firsts were simultaneously present in Suffolk. Name them.

13. Where, in 1985, was Wallcreeper last recorded in Britain?

14. What bird, a first for Britain, confused all those who saw it at Spurn Point on 27th April 1984 and the record was not submitted to the British Birds Rarities Committee until 2000?

15. On 8th–9th June 1984 Britain's first twitchable Bridled Tern was present here, at Rutland Water. As a result of this twitch, who made the pages of *British Birds* magazine for all the wrong reasons?

16. Which North African species made its second appearance in the UK in 1984 at Portland, 101 years after it was first recorded in Nottinghamshire?

17. Of seven Nearctic landbirds recorded in Scilly in October 1985, there were two closely related non-passerines. Name both for one point.

18. What did the observers of Britain's first Savannah (Ipswich) Sparrow at Portland Bill in April 1982 believe it to be?

19. Which rarity was recorded 35 times in the 1980s, but only twice previously?

20. Which 1980 UK 'first', seen on Fair Isle, was subsequently usurped as a first by a 1975 record at Holkham, Norfolk?

RARE BIRDS IN THE UNITED ARAB EMIRATES
Nick Moran – OSME

Answers: page 277

1. Which waterbird has only been recorded once in UAE, at Al Warsan Lakes, but stayed for over five years between 2002 and 2008?

2. With what species did the long-staying Red-knobbed Coot hybridise?

3. Which species was recorded for the first and only time in April 2004, in Safa Park with a flock of Hobbies?

4. Where was the UAE's first Ashy Drongo found in December 2006?

5. Name the species seen on 26th April this year at Mushrif Palace Garden which would be a first for UAE, if accepted, by the Emirates Bird Records Committee (EBRC).

6. Which species was considered an uncommon migrant and winter visitor until this year, when breeding was proved at Al Ghazal Golf Club?

7. Which rare seabird, the only UAE record, was found in luxury accommodation in October 2004?

8. Name one of the two species of wader, formerly considered to be winter visitors or uncommon migrants, but that were proved to be breeding in 1996.

9. How many birders, according to Club 300, have seen more than 400 species?

10. Red-footed Booby has only occurred once, in 1979, but how was it travelling?

11. Which addition to the UAE list was seen at Al Wathba Lake between 3rd and 12th January this year (2010)?

12. As of 17th July 2010, how many species had been recorded in the UAE?

13. Which species was recorded for the first and only time in 1969, having been apparently 'aeroplane assisted'?

14. What species, seen at Safa Park in December 2008, was not only a new bird for UAE but also for Arabia?

15. The first breeding record in UAE of which species was claimed in June this year?

16. Which species has one record involving five adults and one juvenile in January 2003?

17. What is the only eagle of the genus *Haliaeetus* to be recorded in the UAE?

18. Name the species heard, but not seen, in April this year on the Kalba Plain, which would be a first for UAE if accepted by the EBRC.

19. Which starling species has only been recorded once in UAE?

20. What is the scientific name of the endemic taxon of Collared Kingfisher?

THE LARKS OF THE WORLD
Paul Donald – OBC

Answers: page 277

1. Which lark species breeds in Kazakhstan and occurs, but is not known to breed, in the United Arab Emirates and was recorded on Scilly in 1985?

2. Which of the following larks do not exist: Black Lark, Red Lark, Rusty Lark and the Navy Lark?

3. Which flower is named after a feature of lark anatomy?

4. What is special about the *peregrina* race of *Eremophilia alpestris* (Horned Lark)?

5. Which southern African species of lark always lays just one egg?

6. Which Critically Endangered lark is restricted to a range of just 7 square km?

7. Name the other two Critically Endangered larks.

8. Which lark is named after a celestial object (apart from the sky)?

9. Which of the six species of Long-billed Larks *Certhilauda* does not occur in South Africa?

10. Which lark species, discovered in 1955, and endemic to northern Kenya, is found in two disjunct populations?

11. What is the connection between Williams's Lark and Oakham?

12. How many races of Shore Lark does the *Handbook of the Birds of the World* (*HBW*) recognise?

13. Which Ethiopian endemic lark has recently been lumped with Gillett's Lark?

14. Name the two species of *Heteromirafra* larks.

15. Horned Lark breeds at 5,400 m at the snow line in which country?

16. Where would you be if you flushed an apparent Spike-heeled Lark in Eastern Africa?

17. What species would it be?

18. What is the connection between an ornithologist, soldier, spy and fraudster and a dark taxon of an *Ammomanes* lark found in Jordan?

19. Do male or female Raso Larks have the longer bill?

20. After who, where or what is the Thekla Lark named?

BREEDING BIRDS OF THE UNITED ARAB EMIRATES
Oscar Campbell – OSME

Answers: page 277

1. Which lark species breeds in both Kazakhstan and the United Arab Emirates, but was not recorded in Britain until 1992 at Portland Bill?

2. Which species has small breeding populations in the Galapagos, Mexico, the Canaries and the South Atlantic as well as the UAE?

3. Which species was recently satellite-tracked from its UAE colony to the Seychelles?

4. What are the two islands where the main breeding colonies of Crab Plover are found?

5. Which species finally bred successfully at Al Wathba Lake in 1998/99, the first successful breeding in Arabia since 1922?

6. What is the Arabic name of the Hoopoe?

7. What subspecies of Southern Grey Shrike commonly breeds in the region?

8. What resident species is Mushrif National Park especially renowned for, with at least four breeding pairs?

9. The UAE forms part of how many Endemic Bird Areas?

10. What is the Arabic species 'al tummeir al asiawi'?

11. Where does the Yellow-throated Sparrow winter?

12. Where was Caspian Tern first proved to breed in the UAE in 1995?

13. Which famous ornithologist developed his 'Handicap Principle' from his detailed studies of the Arabian Babbler?

14. The Yasat Islands qualify as an Important Bird Area because of their breeding populations of three species. Name two.

15. Which common migrant and winter visitor is said to have bred annually prior to 1927 on the lighthouse buildings on Greater Tunb Island?

16. Which species was first confirmed to breed in the UAE in 1990 at Khatt in Ra's al-Khaimah and appeared to constitute the only breeding station in the entire Arabian peninsula?

17. How many species of the genus *Merops* are known to have bred in UAE?

18. Bifasciated Lark is the old name for which species?

19. The naturalist Hemprich is commemorated by which bird name?

20. What is the average clutch size for Chestnut-bellied Sandgrouse?

BIRDING IN BRITAIN IN THE 1980s
Chris Balchin – NBC

Answers: page 278

1. Which lark breeds in Kazakhstan, probably breeds in the United Arab Emirates and was recorded an average of 13 times per year in Britain in the 1980s?

2. Which rare vagrant shared top billing in Dorset with the Radipole Lake Pied-billed Grebe in January 1980?

3. Which wader was added to the British List through a sighting in South Wales on 30th August 1982?

4. Who became Chairman of the Rare Breeding Birds Panel in 1983 and continued in that role to the end of the decade?

5. In what year did Little Bitterns breed at Potteric Carr?

6. What item on the menu at Nancy's Café was named after the elderly waitress who worked there in the 1980s?

7. Which two current editors of a well-known birding journal had a first for Britain in June 1981. For an extra point name the bird.

8. Why was news of the Tengmalm's Owl at Spurn in March 1983 suppressed?

9. What was the other big suppression in the 1980s of a species that has not returned since?

10. Huge numbers of twitchers flocked to North Ronaldsay in June 1988 to see which species, which subsequently proved to be a waste of money?

11. Which Mediterranean warbler was a first for the UK in 1982?

12. Which species had 17 records in 1979, and then over 17,000 in 1980?

13. Who famously 'called the waders' and made the top ten of listing twitchers in 1982?

14. What bird at Ballycotton Marsh, Co Cork, from 7th February to 3rd April 1981, and described in *British Birds* as 'much twitched but rather boring', was not seen in Great Britain until 1996 (at Stodmarsh)?

15. What species was plucked from a mist-net at Damerham in Hampshire on 23 September 1980 – only the second for mainland Britain?

16. To the nearest £100, how much did a top of the range Kowa TSN Fluorite telescope cost with 20–60 zoom in 1987?

17. Which well known bird artist associated with north-east England, but born in Kettering, died in 1981?

18. Approximately how many records of Little Egret were accepted by the British Birds Rarities Committee in 1989 – to the nearest 10?

19. In 1984 the RSPB acquired its 100th bird reserve. What was its name?

20. Which rare vagrant was identified from a photograph at Wilstone Reservoir, Tring, on 9th November 1981?

BIRDS OF KAZAKHSTAN
Steve Rooke – ABC

Answers: page 278

1. Which lark species breeds in both Kazakhstan and the United Arab Emirates and was recorded once in Britain in the 1980s on Bardsey in 1982?

2. Who wrote the standard work *The Birds of Kazakhstan* (1960–74).

3. Name the three Critically Endangered species that are listed as having occurred in Kazakhstan.

4. Which race of Pander's Ground-jay occurs only in the South Balkhash Desert?

5. Who is the BirdLife partner in Kazakhstan?

6. What bird is depicted on ACBK's logo?

7. The famous Chokpak ringing station is only effective for trapping and visible migration in the autumn period with one particular weather condition. What is that?

8. A Sociable Lapwing called Erzhan was tracked by satellite for three consecutive years from its breeding grounds in Kazakhstan to its wintering grounds in which country?

9. Why did the breeding population of Yellow-eyed Stock Dove decline sharply in 1973–74?

10. What is the total bird species list for Kazakhstan?

11. The Relict Gull breeds in Kazakhstan and how many other countries?

12. It is generally considered that the *vittata* form of Pied Wheatear, which breeds in Kazakhstan, is a colour morph, but what does E. N. Panov believe its origin to be?

13. Which European explorer, born in 1794, has his name commemorated in two Kazakh birds and an endemic hamster?

14. How many Important Bird Areas are there in Kazakhstan?

15. What species, known in Kazakhstan from a misidentified museum specimen in 1900, was rediscovered in Thailand in 2006 and found breeding in Afghanistan in 2009?

16. Of which Kazakhstan species is 'Silly Borat tweeted' an anagram?

17. What race of Greater Sandplover breeds in Kazakhstan?

18. How many species of Wheatear can be found in Kazakhstan?

19. The Korgalzhyn and Naurzum Nature Reserves were recognised with which international designation in 2008?

20. When did Kazakhstan become a contracting member to the Ramsar Convention?

BIRDS OF HAMPSHIRE
John Clark – ABC

Answers: page 279

1. Who wrote *Birds of Hampshire* published in 1993?

2. In which decade was Gilbert White's *The Natural History of Selborne* first published?

3. Where was Hampshire's only Lanceolated Warbler caught and ringed?

4. Which member of the heron family (in Category A on the Hampshire list) is a homophone of an ancient Hampshire village?

5. Both Hampshire's American Bitterns occurred in the same year – which year?

6. From what fate was the 1990 Baillion's Crake at Normandy Marsh, Lymington, rescued?

7. Hampshire produced the first UK breeding record for Firecrest in which year?

8. A nestling Montagu's Harrier was ringed in the New Forest in Hampshire in 1952 and turned up 1 year 10 months and 18 days later 354 km away. Where?

9. The seven Little Bustard records for Hampshire span 180 years. How many of these were in the last century?

10. With which American president did Lord Grey of Fallodon go birdwatching along the Itchen in 1910?

11. How many Goshawks were ringed in Hampshire in 2011?

12. In which year was American Redstart recorded in Hampshire?

13. In which year was Hampshire's first record of Franklin's Gull?

14. How was Hampshire's sole White-throated Needletail record verified?

15. In the Hampshire Biodiversity Action Plan, section 1.2 Priority Shorebirds, there were three priority scarce breeding species. Name two.

16. In 2011 were more Chiffchaffs, Blackcaps or Sedge Warblers ringed in Hampshire?

17. On 14th October 1962 a Dark-eyed Junco, a Song Sparrow and two White-throated Sparrows were all found on which liner at Southampton?

18. Name another North American passerine that has been recorded on a liner at Southampton docks.

19. Pallas's Sandgrouse was recorded in Hampshire in two different years, separated by exactly two decades. What were the years?

20. A kingfisher trapped at Southampton Docks on 20th Oct 1983 had been ringed abroad. Where?

THE STATE OF THE UK'S BIRDS
Andy Clements – BTO

Answers: page 279

1. What was the predecessor to the Breeding Bird Survey?

2. In which year was *The State of the UK's Birds* first published?

3. What caused a hiatus in monitoring in 2001?

4. What important new aspect was introduced in *The State of the UK's Birds 2002*, enlarging the scope of the annual report?

5. The RSPB's *State of the UK Birds 2011* helped mark which 40th anniversary?

6. The first ever national survey of which species was carried out in 2011?

7. In *The State of the UK's Birds 2001*, which iconic species was highlighted as likely to suffer as an indirect effect of 'closing the countryside' due to the foot-and-mouth epidemic among cattle?

8. In *The State of the UK's Birds 2008*, for which species was a Species Recovery Project in England announced?

9. The cover of the 2011 *State of the UK's Birds* featured a Common Eider, which is known as holding which avian record, arguably?

10. Which common British breeding species underwent the largest percentage increase in the 40 years to 2009?

11. Which waterbird has the lowest UK wintering population?

12. Name one of the two newly documented threats to the UK Nightjars' breeding success.

13. Which species, which colonised the UK naturally about 40 years ago, now has almost 2,000 singing males in summer?

14. How many booming Bitterns were recorded in 2007?

15. Which British breeding species underwent the largest percentage decrease in both the 15 and 40 year period to 2009?

16. Which duck species breeding numbers fell by 45% between a survey in 1995 and the next one in 2007?

17. In *The State of the UK's Birds 2011*, Henderson Island, in addition to being the only known breeding site of Henderson Petrel, also has four endemic bird species. Name them.

18. How many *State of the UK's Birds* reports had been published prior to that for 2011?

19. Which British breeding species in the UK Biodiversity Action Plan underwent a 90% population decrease in the 14 years up to 2009?

20. In *The State of the UK's Birds 2005*, what inaccessible (in two senses) species was highlighted as being a particular UK responsibility?

BRITISH BIRDS OF PREY
Graham Madge – OBC

Answers: page 279

1. The common names of three British breeding birds of prey begin with the letter H. Name them.

2. Which breeding British eagle lays spotted eggs?

3. Who did a long-term study of Common Buzzards in the New Forest and published his results in *The Buzzard* in 1974?

4. Britain's oldest recorded wild bird of prey reached the ripe old age of 25 years, 6 months and 26 days. Name the species.

5. The genus of Osprey and the species name of Eurasian Sparrowhawk derive from two figures of Greek mythology. What was the relationship of the two figures?

6. Name a species which exhibits polygyny in its breeding.

7. How many species of breeding raptor winter in sub-Saharan Africa?

8. Which is the only breeding British bird of prey that does not have yellow feet?

9. The author of the 1976 New Naturalist title *British Birds of Prey*, by his own admission, had no expertise in UK birds of prey. On which continent was his raptor expertise gained?

10. UK breeding Hobbies are believed to migrate to the Zambezi Basin, but where were the wintering grounds of radio-tracked birds that had bred near Berlin?

11. In the most recently published account of Rare Breeding Birds in the UK, for 2012, published in *British Birds*, name the two English counties that held the highest total of confirmed breeding pairs of Goshawk.

12. Name two authors who have contributed volumes on birds of prey to the Poyser monograph series.

13. What colour is the iris of an adult Buzzard?

14. Which Oxford educated Aberdonian learned forest management in Russia, served as a recruiter for the Coast-watch Service in World War I and became an early authority on the Golden Eagle (and the bagpipes)?

15. In most raptor species, females weigh more than males. Which British breeding species has the lowest percentage differences between average mass of males and females?

16. Which two species were conclusively proved to have bred in Scotland in 1990 and 1994 respectively for the first time since the 19th century?

17. Two British breeding birds of prey show a blue-grey cere in adult plumage. Name one of them.

18. Which British bird of prey has the longest incubation period at 43–45 days?

19. Records of six species of falcon are subject to assessment by the British Birds Rarities Committee. Name three.

20. The *Hand-List of British Birds*, 1912 (Hartert, Jourdain, Ticehurst & Witherby), described *Falco regulus* as resident; what is the unchanged English name of that species?

AFGHANISTAN BIRDS
Mike Blair – OSME

Answers: page 280

1. What is the national bird of Afghanistan?

2. The OSME logo features one of the five sandgrouse species found in Afghanistan. What was its old name?

3. Name two of the three Critically Endangered species on the Afghanistan list.

4. Spell Ménétriés's ('manytrees'), as in Ménétriés's Warbler.

5. The Sinai Rosefinch of the Middle East has an endemic and disjunct subspecies in central Afghanistan. Who is it named after?

6. Apart from eye and eye-ring colour, what is the key plumage feature that separates Yellow-eyed Pigeon from Stock Dove?

7. Which is the only single-species wader family found in Afghanistan?

8. The Afghan Snowfinch is almost endemic, although there is a non-breeding record from which other country?

9. What is the full name of the entomologist whose first name is commemorated in the scientific name of the Afghan Snowfinch?

10. What does the Royal Australian Air Force use Herons and Kestrels for in Afghanistan?

11. Which two sandgrouse species recorded in Afghanistan have bright white bellies?

12. Name the two pratincole species that have been recorded in Afghanistan.

13. Which race of Ashy Drongo, recently recorded in the Western Palearctic in United Arab Emirates and Kuwait, breeds in Afghanistan?

14. Which species, known only from a single specimen collected in India in the 19th century, was discovered breeding in the Wakhan corridor of eastern Afghanistan in 2008?

15. In what decade was that first bird collected?

16. The three principal colour morphs of Variable Wheatear are usually considered to represent three different subspecies. Name two (scientific trinomials only).

17. How many species of *Aquila* eagle have been recorded Afghanistan?

18. After which British natural historian was Rufous-breasted Accentor formerly named (and is still named in the trinomial)?

19. How many species of lark breed in Afghanistan?

20. Name three of the five accentor species recorded in Afghanistan.

BIRDS NEW TO BRITAIN
1980–2004
Adrian Pitches – OBC

Answers: page 280

1. Which Nearctic species triggered a mass twitch in 1989?

2. Which Pacific species was a surprising first for the British Isles in 1990 and ended up returning in the following two years?

3. Which species was a mystery for over three years and was seen and captured several times before being officially identified?

4. In total, how many firsts in this period were found from December to February?

5. What bird (considered to be a first at the time) did African Bird Club trustees not see because they loyally attended their council meeting in London on Saturday 7th June 2003 rather than go twitching?

6. 1981 and 1982 were considered the two golden years. In total, how many firsts were discovered in those two years (excluding the Long-toed Stint)?

7. According to the book *Birds New to Britain 1980–2004*, which notable ornithologist made the suggestion in 1955 that Hume's Yellow-browed Warbler was a future contender for the British List?

8. The first Hume's Yellow-browed Warbler was eventually seen in 1966, but how many years passed before the story was written up in *British Birds* magazine?

9. Which bird new to Britain between 1980 and 2004 breeds the closest to Britain?

10. Which month of the year was the best for finding firsts?

11. Which Mediterranean first for the UK lingered for a long time in spring 1982?

12. Which Norfolk mega stayed for a long time but was still very hard to twitch?

13. Who was the first to suggest correctly that a strange-looking lark discovered at Portland Bill by a YOC group in May 1992 might be a Lesser Short-toed Lark?

14. How many firsts in this period were found on the Scillies?

15. How many birds that were newly added to the Irish List between 1980 and 2004 have subsequently been accepted onto the British list?

16. Which 1987 first for Britain has subsequently been recorded in Ireland but never again in Britain?

17. How many firsts were there in 1993?

18. How many new Nearctic warblers were found? Name three of them.

19. Which bird new to Britain between 1980 and 2004 had the highest number of accepted records by the end of 2011 (according to the British Birds Rarities Committee report for that year)?

20. Excluding Fair Isle, how many firsts were found in Shetland?

POPULATION ESTIMATES FOR BIRDS OF BRITAIN
Andy Musgrove – BTO

Answers: page 281

1. What is the most abundant wintering bird that has never bred in Britain?

2. How many races of wren breed in Britain?

3. Which Auk species is estimated to have 20,000 more birds in the breeding season in the UK than in GB? (Great Britain is England, Wales and Scotland, whereas the United Kingdom is England, Wales, Scotland and Northern Ireland. The Isle of Man is part of neither but its avifauna is sometimes included, and sometimes not.)

4. List Britain's woodpeckers, excluding vagrants, in order of ascending abundance.

5. What is the most common breeding species in Britain?

6. What was the estimated population in the breeding season of St Kilda Wren in 1993?

7. What is Britain's commonest breeding seabird?

8. What is the most abundant species that breeds in only one of the UK's four nations?

9. List our four commonest breeding thrushes in order of descending abundance.

10. What is our rarest regularly breeding warbler?

11. What was the estimated population of White-tailed Eagles in the breeding season in 1800?

12. What is the total number of species ever recorded in Britain?

13. What is Britain's commonest corvid?

14. Which species was estimated as having around 150 breeding pairs in 2002, but around 700 by the period of the latest Avian Populations Estimates Panel paper?

15. How many species of raptors breed in Britain?

16. What is Britain's commonest long-distance summer migrant?

17. What is Britain's commonest nocturnal bird?

18. Which introduced Anatidae species had an estimated population of 2,300 pairs in the breeding season in 1988?

19. Apart from Pheasant, what is the only British non-passerine to have a breeding population in excess of a million pairs?

20. To the nearest million, how many wintering waterbirds does the UK hold?

BIRDS OF SOUTH AFRICA
Adam Riley – ABC

Answers: page 281

1. What is the national bird of South Africa?

2. What is the Afrikaans name for African Penguin?

3. Name the three mousebirds that occur in South Africa.

4. What bird family found in South Africa has one representative species in each of Asia, Africa and America?

5. Which is the only South African bird classified as Critically Endangered?

6. What is the scientific name for the bird family comprising two species endemic to South Africa and Lesotho?

7. How many species of cisticola breed in South Africa?

8. What South African bird's name is an anagram of 'Fatal Action'?

9. When was the first British-ringed Barn Swallow recovered in South Africa?

10. What South African landbird has the largest wingspan?

11. Which common cisticola's name is a combination of two common nicknames?

12. How many BirdLife Endemic Bird Areas are there in South Africa?

13. What bird family found in South Africa has one representative species in each of Australia, Americas, Asia and Africa?

14. Which South African bird's scientific name comes last alphabetically?

15. According to BirdLife International, how many Globally Threatened species occur in South Africa?

16. Apart from Swallow, what is the only other British-ringed passerine to have been recovered in South Africa?

17. Which duck is a vagrant to the Prince Edwards Islands?

18. Which South African endemic is similar to the Andean and Campo Flickers of South America in its behaviour?

19. How many species of lark are endemic to South Africa?

20. Of South Africa's 24 *(now 32)* Endangered and Vulnerable birds, how many are vultures?

DESERT BIRDS OF ISRAEL
Jonathan Meyrav – OSME

Answers: page 281

1. How many eggs do Sandgrouse usually lay?

2. Name the two Critically Endangered birds that occur in Israeli deserts.

3. What bird is also known as Pharoah's chicken?

4. What is the main plumage difference between Houbara and Macqueen's Bustards?

5. How many Important Bird Areas are recognised in Israel?

6. Which is the heaviest sandgrouse species found in Israel?

7. The English name of which desert bird of Israel is an anagram of 'Red Stalker'?

8. To what or whom does Isabelline refer to in Isabelline Wheatear or Shrike?

9. What resident Israeli desert bird is also an indigenous resident to Madagascar?

10. How many other species are still named after the Rev Henry Tristram apart from the Grackle/Starling and what are they?

11. How many races of Sinai Rosefinch are recognised?

12. What Israeli desert bird is named in honour of a French surgeon?

13. Which unlikely desert species was found on the shore of the Dead Sea in February 1963?

14. What Israeli desert bird is named after two English ornithologists – one in its common name and the other in its scientific name?

15. Name one of the two *(three)* Endangered raptor species found in Israel's deserts.

16. What is the IUCN Red List classification for Nubian Nightjar?

17. How many of Israel's wheatears are there on the British List? Name three.

18. What is the average incubation period of Tristram's Grackle/Starling?

19. What bird 'came up at even and covered the camp' of the Children of Israel in Exodus?

20. Which Israeli desert species was recorded as a very rare vagrant to the UK in 1962/63, although it is no longer an Israeli bird due to taxonomic revision?

THE ENDEMIC BIRDS OF MADAGASCAR
Callan Cohen – ABC

Answers: page 282

1. Which bird previously thought to be extinct, was rediscovered at Lake Matsaborimena?

2. The search for which endemic cost the life of the world's first mega-lister?

3. How many of the ten species of duck that occur on Madagascar are endemic?

4. Name them.

5. Name the only endemic species of the family Scolopacidae to occur in Madagascar.

6. Which species' Malagasy name 'voronjaza' means crybaby bird?

7. Which endemic bird's scientific name is *Atelornis pittoides*?

8. Why is the Chabert Vanga so called?

9. How tall was the largest species of the extinct Aepyornithidae or elephant birds, to the nearest metre?

10. Which breeding endemic migrates to the east coast of Africa?

11. Which species of greenbul is now considered to be a Malagasy warbler?

12. What is the clutch size of Humblot's Heron?

13. What colour is the frontal shield of the Madagascar Jacana?

14. Madagascar Turtle Dove is most closely related to which other Indian Ocean pigeon?

15. What are the main items of diet of the Madagascar Serpent-eagle?

16. Which bird's scientific name suggests it is a Madagascan species when it has in fact not been recorded there?

17. What similarity is there between Vasa Parrots and Aquatic Warblers and Red-billed Buffalo-weavers in their mating behaviour?

18. What was the large eagle that became extinct in comparatively recent times and may have contributed to the legend of the Roc in tales of Sinbad the Sailor?

19. What project did the 2003 Birdfair support?

20. Name one of the two endemics that featured on the Birdfair poster in 2003.

PITTAS OF ASIA
Chris Gooddie – OBC

Answers: page 282

1. What is the only species of pitta to breed in Sri Lanka?

2. Which pitta takes its name from a Norfolk-born banker?

3. Which pitta shares its alternative (and specific scientific) names with a leaf-monkey?

4. What is the more commonly used name for the Moluccan Pitta?

5. What is the current IUCN Red List category for Fairy Pitta?

6. Most Asian pittas fall silent while brooding, but which species continues to call?

7. Which Asian pitta lays the largest eggs?

8. The nest and eggs of three Asian pitta species have never been found. Name two.

9. For a bonus, name the third.

10. Which Asian pitta calls like a human wolf whistle?

11. Why is the Banded Pitta's scientific name *Pitta guajana*?

12. What noise do the tiny feet of the Fairy Pitta make?

13. How many pitta species occur in Borneo?

14. What is the origin of the common name 'Pitta'?

15. Which pitta was lost for 52 years until its rediscovery in 1988?

16. What is the highest altitude at which an Asian pitta species has been observed?

17. Who was the first person to use the generic name Pitta for the whole family?

18. Name two of the species of Asian pitta that are true migrants.

19. For which species of pitta is Khao Pra Bang Khram Wildlife Sanctuary in Thailand (aka Khao Nor Chu Chi) best known?

20. Which pitta occurs in South Korea?

STONE-CURLEWS
Neil Calbrade – BTO

Answers: page 283

1. Name a continent with more than three species of stone-curlew?

2. Which thick-knee taxon has recently been elevated to species status by the IOC (International Ornithological Congress) World Bird List?

3. How many races of the stone-curlew are there?

4. The specific name *oedicnemus* refers to which part of the Eurasian stone-curlew?

5. Name one of the two sub-Saharan countries in which British-ringed stone-curlews have been recovered.

6. In 2011 which English county held the most confirmed breeding pairs of Stone-curlew?

7. What is the oldest Stone-curlew recorded in the British ringing scheme?

8. Name one of the two Canary races of Stone-curlew.

9. Where does the Indian Thick-knee migrate to?

10. What is the most northerly recovery of a British-ringed Stone-curlew?

11. When did the Stone-curlew last breed in the Netherlands?

12. In medieval times looking a Stone-curlew in the eye was thought to cure which complaint?

13. Which species of thick-knee frequently nests in association with breeding crocodiles?

14. In which year did Linnaeus describe the Stone-curlew?

15. Which species of stone-curlew sounds like a currant-filled suet pudding?

16. Which thick-knee species has become semi-domesticated to help control insects?

17. What man-made structures do Senegal Thick-knees utilise for nesting?

18. What is the major habitat-selection difference between Beach Thick-knee and Great Thick-knee?

19. What is the Stone-curlew called in Germany?

20. How long is incubation for each egg?

THREATENED WATERFOWL
Nick Acheson – OSME

Answers: page 283

1. In which year was Pink-headed Duck last seen conclusively in the wild (according to BirdLife International)?

2. What is the current IUCN Red List category for Scaly-sided Merganser?

3. Which Endangered hole-nesting Asian duck inhabits stagnant or slow-flowing wetlands in or near forests?

4. How many Critically Endangered waterfowl species are there?

5. Name two.

6. What is the Latin name of Blue Duck?

7. What is the common name of the extinct flightless merganser from New Zealand?

8. What is the name of the White-headed Duck's display in which it raises its head high and cocks its tail?

9. What type of habitat does the Salvadori's Teal prefer?

10. Within five years, when was the Chubut or White-headed Steamerduck first described?

11. In what year was the last confirmed sighting of Crested Shelduck?

12. According to Kear, the last sighting of Crested Shelduck was in 1971, although this is debatable. In which country was it?

13. Prior to its rediscovery in 2006, in what year was the last previous recorded sighting of the Madagascar Pochard?

14. For which Critically Endangered duck is the brine-fly *Scatella sexnotata* an important prey species?

15. Which Vulnerable duck shares its name with a British racing driver who won Le Mans in 1959?

16. What is the name of the mountain range in the Russian far east where most of the world's Scaly-sided Merganser breed?

17. What population process is limiting the Madagascar Pochard population to around 25 birds and what is causing this?

18. What is the name of the main site for Brazilian Merganser?

19. In which Brazilian state is it located?

20. According to Hoogerwerf, how much does a male White-winged Duck weigh in grammes, to the nearest 200 g?

BIRDS IN THE MUSIC OF OLIVIER MESSIAEN
Tom McKinney – OSME

Answers: page 283

1. In *Réveil des oiseaux*, which bird is represented by piccolo doubled by cor anglais?

2. Which man-made object interrupts the Curlew in *Catalogue d'oiseaux*?

3. *Réveil des oiseaux* was Messaien's first piece dedicated almost entirely to birdsong. Where is the piece set?

4. How many birds are there in *Catalogue d'oiseaux* for piano written in 1958?

5. Which bird in the music of Olivier Messiaen would be most likely to be seen at Annapurna base camp at 4,000 m above sea level in the Himalayas?

6. Apart from Alpine Chough, which other bird in *Catalogue d'oiseaux* is not on the British List?

7. Which species did Messiaen describe as 'perhaps the loveliest singer in France'?

8. Messiaen's biographer Peter Hill gave the composer a copy of *Birds of Great Britain* written by which famous 19th century ornithologist?

9. Which bird in the music of Olivier Messiaen is the most threatened?

10. In which Messiaen piece does birdsong first make an appearance?

11. Which Messiaen piece was premiered on 7th August at the 2015 BBC Proms?

12. What is the English name of the species featured in *La Fauvette passerinette*?

13. Name one of the two species – one Asian and one North American – that inspired Messiaen's 'Interstellar call' written for solo horn?

14. In the antistrophes of *Chronochromie*, the Skylark is represented by which two percussion instruments?

15. Which bird opens the piece *Oiseaux exotiques*?

16. Name two North American landbirds which feature in Messiaen's 1974 work 'From the Canyons to the Stars', and which have occurred as vagrants in the UK.

17. Act 2 Scene 6 of which opera is entitled *Sermon to the Birds*?

18. Which bird features in *Quatuor pour la fin du temps*?

19. The song of which New Caledonian bird is associated with the Angel in *Saint François d'Assise*?

20. Name one of the three instruments used in the Gerygone's song in *Saint François d'Assise*.

RARE BIRDS IN BRITAIN
IN THE 1980s
Stuart Elsom – OBC

Answers: page 284

1. In 1986, which species recorded an unprecedented influx of eight birds to Scilly, one of which was taken by a cat, and another drowned by a wave?

2. Of the six Black-billed Cuckoos that occurred in the 1980s, how many were found dead?

3. Why is the period 6th to 27th March 1983 still notorious among twitchers?

4. A nest and two eggs of which Nearctic species turned up in Montrose, Angus, in 1983?

5. In which two years in the 1980s was Albert the Black-browed Albatross absent from Hermaness?

6. From 11th to 16th April 1982 Britain's first Savannah Sparrow was present at Portland Bill, Dorset. What species did the first observers of the bird consider it likely to be?

7. What Nearctic passerine was found freshly dead at Wembury, South Devon, on 22 October 1985?

8. Which bird, recorded in Britain only twice, was found in June 1984, 101 years after the first record?

9. How many species of *Catharus* thrush were seen on Scilly in the 1980s?

10. Where was the only record of Wallcreeper in Britain in the 1980s?

11. What was the last new addition to the British List in the 1980s?

12. Which year saw a mini-invasion of nutcrackers?

13. What links Yellow-browed Bunting, Long-toed Stint and Blackburnian Warbler?

14. How many Nearctic wood-warblers were added to the British list in the 1980s?

15. Where was the 1987 Dusky Thrush seen?

16. Which two counties recorded Cliff Swallows in the 1980s?

17. What links St. Agnes, St. Mary's, Barnstaple and Red Rocks in the Wirral?

18. What first for Britain was present in Sumburgh, Shetland, between 30th September and 2nd October 1985, exactly the same dates as Ireland's first Short-billed Dowitcher was present in County Wexford at Tacumshin?

19. Was White's Thrush or Siberian Thrush more common in the 1980s?

20. What highly sought-after species drifted along the coast at Llanfairfechan, Caernarfonshire, on 3rd September 1989?

NOTABLE FEMALE FIGURES IN BIRDING
Fiona Barclay – BTO

Answers: page 284

1. How many female members have there been on the British Birds Rarities Committee?

2. Who was the lead co-ordinator of the BTO Atlas 2007–11?

3. Name the eminent scientist, Director of Conservation at WWT, who has worked on the Madagascar Pochard, Bewick's Swan and, most recently, the project to save the Spoon-billed Sandpiper.

4. Which Duchess became the RSPB's first president?

5. How many women have been President of the RSPB?

6. Which woman wrote the Poyser monograph *Bewick's Swan*?

7. Who was the aptly named lady proprietor of the famous birder's café in Cley, North Norfolk, in the 1970s and 1980s?

8. Which distinguished Welsh ornithologist was captured by Ethiopian rebels in 1976 and held captive for eight months?

9. On the trip to Madagascar in 1999 where she died in a vehicle accident, what was the final bird Phoebe Snetsinger added to her record-breaking world list?

10. Name the ornithologist, famed for her work on brood parasites, who is married to Tim Dee, author of *The Running Sky*?

11. Who, until April (2015), was the President of the British Ornithologists' Union?

12. In which year did Emily Williamson found The Plumage League, which later became the RSPB?

13. Name one of the two women on the team of 24 ornithologists who edited *The Birds of the Western Palearctic* in nine volumes between 1977 and 1994.

14. Who illustrated the Helm family guides to *Wildfowl* and *Crows and Jays*?

15. Who was the cousin (once-removed) of Richard Meinertzhagen who became a world authority on *Mallophaga* or bird lice?

16. Who was the first female President of the British Ornithologists' Union?

17. Which woman influenced many older birders by writing *The Observer's Book of British Birds* in 1937?

18. Which woman wrote the Poyser monograph *The Barn Swallow*?

19. Who, with Alan Harris, co-illustrated the groundbreaking *Macmillan Field Guide to Bird Identification*?

20. Who was the only female President of the BTO?

THE ENDEMIC BIRDS OF SAO TOME
Tom Lewis – ABC

Answers: page 284

1. Which three endemic species or subspecies are Critically Endangered?

2. Which top ten world lister was part of the group of birders who rediscovered the São Tomé Grosbeak in 1991?

3. What colour is the vent on a Giant Sunbird?

4. Which endemic species is a frequent host for the African Emerald Cuckoo?

5. Which is the only nocturnal endemic species to have ever featured on a São Tomé stamp?

6. Why is the population of São Tomé Prinia thought to be increasing?

7. Which Portuguese explorer and naturalist, who died in 1909, is honoured in the names of two São Tomé endemics?

8. Which endemic occupies the behavioural niche of treecreeper or nuthatch?

9. How many endemic birds in São Tomé have *thomensis* as the second part of their scientific binomial?

10. Which species of quail is represented by an endemic subspecies on São Tomé?

11. The São Tomé Short-tail has apparently abandoned areas of habitat near Bombaim, after the locality began to be heavily used for harvesting which alcoholic beverage?

12. What is an alternative common name for the São Tomé Short-tail?

13. According to BirdLife International, what is the main reason for the decline of the São Tomé Green-pigeon?

14. What colour are the tips of the tail feathers on a male São Tomé Oriole?

15. The São Tomé Ibis is also known by what other English name?

16. São Tomé Kingfisher is considered by some taxonomists to be a subspecies of which kingfisher on the African mainland?

17. What colour is the bill of both sexes of the São Tomé Oriole?

18. Who first published his description of the Dwarf Olive Ibis in 1923?

19. What does *crassirostris* mean in the scientific name of São Tomé Oriole?

20. What is the favoured food of São Tomé Green-pigeon?

FLUFFTAILS OF THE WORLD
John Kinghorn - ABC

Answers: page 285

1. How many of the nine species of flufftail do not occur in the southern hemisphere?

2. Hackett *et al.* in 2008 suggested that flufftails were not as closely related to rails as previously thought and they considered them to be more closely related to which non-rail family?

3. Which sex builds the nest of the Madagascar Flufftail?

4. Which animal frequently preys heavily on Buff-spotted Flufftails, particularly in residential areas?

5. Which flufftail's scientific name suggests it is the most beautiful of the family?

6. Only two flufftail species have an IUCN threat status more serious than Least Concern. Name them.

7. Apart from spots, what links White-spotted and Buff-spotted Flufftails?

8. What colour are flufftail eggs (or, at least, those that have been studied)?

9. How many Critically Endangered White-winged Flufftails did Greg Davies succeed in flushing during a year's survey of high-altitude African marshes in 2013–14?

10. Which Madagascan nature reserve has proved to be the most fruitful spot in recent years for birders seeking the Slender-billed Flufftail?

11. Which is the only flufftail to be found in Senegal?

12. Which flufftail species has a song that according to local legend is 'the wail of a banshee, or the noise made by a chameleon in the agonies of giving birth, or the sound of a chameleon mourning for his mother, whom he has killed in an argument over some mushrooms'?

13. What is the Afrikaans name for White-winged Flufftail?

14. Which is the only flufftail *definitely* known to be a regular intra-African migrant?

15. In South Africa the call of the White-winged Flufftail is said to be very similar to the roosting call of which large southern African bird?

16. How many species of flufftail have been seen in Namibia?

17. Which flufftail is also known as Waters's Flufftail?

18. How many different colour descriptors feature in the English names of flufftails?

19. According to BirdLife International, which flufftail has the largest range?

20. Which is the heaviest of the flufftail species occurring in South Africa?

SONGS AND CALLS OF EUROPEAN BIRDS
Stephen McAvoy – BTO

Answers: page 285

1. Which widespread European corvid has the lowest frequency call of all the European crow species?

2. Which British bird is traditionally said to 'change its tune in June'?

3. Intergrades between Common Chiffchaff and Iberian Chiffchaff often feature elements of both species' songs. What is the name commonly given to these intergrades?

4. Which European sea-duck's display call sounds remarkably like a scandalised old lady?!

5. Which aquatic species is known for 'sharming'?

6. The famous parson-naturalist Gilbert White recognised in 1789 that three European warblers *looked* very similar to one another but *sounded* very different. Name the three species that he was able to separate by voice.

7. Which British breeding species has the lowest frequency vocalisation?

8. Which British breeding species goes by the local name of Wailing Heath Chicken, on account of its eerie, far-carrying calls?

9. What was the first trans-Saharan migrant that was found to mimic African birds?

10. Name two of the three birds represented in the 2nd movement of Beethoven's Sixth Symphony, *The Pastoral*.

11. Is the wing-clapping sound Red-necked Nightjars produced by claps above or below the back?

12. How is the song of the Cyprus Scops Owl different from Eurasian Scops Owl?

13. To which bird does the following entry in Witherby's *Handbook of British Birds* refer: 'Only note recorded was a low croak'?

14. If you thought you'd heard a curlew in the mountains of southwestern Russia, what was it likely to have been (if it was not a curlew)?

15. The song of which species inspired the poet John Keats to write 'Thou wast not born for death, immortal Bird!' in his famous ode?

16. Part of which European bird's song has been compared to the sound of a bottle of champagne being opened?

17. Vaughan Williams composed a piece in praise of the song of which bird?

18. Who was the German born pioneer of British bird song recording?

19. Which one of a trio of closely related plovers has a very similar flight call to Spotted Redshank?

20. Which species (whose name suggests it should say nothing at all) actually has a wide range of vocalisations including an explosive, snorting 'heeorr', a gull-like 'ga-oh' and a 'mean, snake-like hissing'?

ENDEMIC BIRDS OF SUMATRA
Ashley Banwell – OBC

Answers: page 285

1. What colour is the throat of a Spot-necked Bulbul?

2. The Enggano White-eye is found on the island of Enggano and the tiny satellite island of Dua – and where else?

3. Name one Critically Endangered endemic Sumatran species.

4. Name one of the three other names that the *Handbook of Birds of the World* gives for Cream-striped Bulbul.

5. Which Sumatran endemic has a call that is very similar to that of Siberian Thrush?

6. Who discovered and named Roll's Partridge?

7. What difference is there in the call of Roll's Partridge and that of the Sumatran Partridge?

8. Which species was Sumatran Drongo formerly lumped with?

9. How many endemic subspecies of Island Thrush are found on Sumatra?

10. Which endemic is known from four specimens?

11. Which is the larger of the two endemic Wren-babblers?

12. How would you describe or demonstrate the song of the Rusty-breasted Wren-babbler ?

13. What tactic do Leafbirds use to deter predators when caught?

14. What colour is the post-ocular stripe on the adult Graceful Pitta?

15. Name two endemic Sumatran species found only on off-shore islands and not on mainland Sumatra?

16. What is the current BirdLife status of Simeulue Scops Owl?

17. The nest of which Sumatran endemic is known from only one example found in 1933?

18. Prior to its rediscovery in 1988, when was Schneider's Pitta last seen, give or take five years?

19. Swiss zoologist Johann Buettikofer is commemorated in the scientific name of which Sumatran endemic?

20. Prior to a sighting in 1997, when was Sumatran Ground Cuckoo last seen?

RARE BIRDS IN ISRAEL FROM 1985 TO THE PRESENT DAY
Yoav Perlman – OSME

Answers: page 286

1. Which Israeli rarity, the fifth to have occurred in the country, was seen at Eilat Beach on 7th May 2016 and grippingly, landed only briefly on the beach, before subsequently giving more prolonged views flying back and forth over the gulf?

2. In 1989 a large-scale arrival of Dunn's Lark occurred in Israel. In what year did the second large-scale arrival occur, with around 20 singing males noted at a single site?

3. Which first for Israel in March 1994 initially baffled the finder, not least because it was, in his own words, 'small and bright green'?

4. How many Velvet Scoters were seen in Jaffa Port on 31st January 2008?

5. Which species occurred for the 11th time in Israel in August 2014 but has only ever been found in a mist-net, never yet independently in the field?

6. Which species, recorded in Beer Sheva in December 2014, came to light when a non-birder caught it in his living room and sent a photograph to a birding friend. who posted it on Facebook?

7. Two ducks seen on a flooded field near Meitzar, Golan, on 8th February 2008 were the first sighting in Israel for 18 years of which species?

8. What was especially significant about the 2016 record of Oriental Turtle Dove on 6th May, Israel's 13th?

9. Which species of bird of prey killed Israel's first Snow Bunting?

10. The sole Western Palaearctic record of what bird species was present in April–May 1998?

11. Why do Mr Rami Mizrachi (on 471 species) and Mr Barak Granit (on 467 species) STILL have bigger Israeli lists than you (Yoav Perlman) (on only 463 species)?

12. According to the finder, James Smith, why did Israel's first confirmed Bean Goose, seen on 14th March 2007 off Eilat's North Beach, depart so quickly inland?

13. Which sporting location subsequently hosted the same Bean Goose two days later?

14. Ornithologists announced in 2015 that Blue-cheeked Bee-eaters had nested in the Negev at Yerucham for the first time in many years, but a local lady had photographic proof that they had nested some years earlier than this. When?

15. How many accepted records of Rough-legged Buzzard have there been after 1985?

16. How many Pallas's Warblers were noted in Israel in the 1990s?

17. What new species to Israel was discovered in the Gan Shmuel kibbutz in December 2014?

18. Which passerine recorded at Jaffa Port on 25th April 2016 was only the third for the Mediterranean zone, and the latest ever recorded?

19. When was Red-throated Diver last recorded in Israel?

20. In autumn 1998 you (i.e. Yoav) were ringing at Kfar Ruppin when you trapped a sixth for Israel. What was the species?

ENDEMIC BIRDS OF BORNEO
Ashley Banwell – OBC

Answers: page 286

1. Name the endemic bird whose generic name in Greek means (roughly) 'suffering from dandruff'.

2. Which species described from a specimen collected in Kalimantan in the 1840s has gone unrecorded for longer than any other in Asia?

3. What is the current IUCN Red List classification of the Black-browed Babbler?

4. Which two features would you use to separate Whitehead's and Hose's Broadbills from one another?

5. Name two Bornean endemics whose common name celebrates John Whitehead's surname.

6. In addition to the three species named after John Whitehead in their common name, two others are named after him and his father in their scientific names. Name one.

7. In which decade did John Whitehead collect in Borneo?

8. How many endemic barbets are there?

9. With which species was the Bornean Ground Cuckoo considered to be conspecific?

10. Pygmy White-eye has recently undergone a change of genus in the HBW checklist, because it was found to be imbedded in a clade of *Lophozosterops* for which its new generic name has priority. From what genus to what?

11. Which two striking features do male and female Bulwer's Pheasants share?

12. One of the endemic Bornean Pheasants and Partridges is in its own genus. Which is it?

13. Which plumage feature distinguishes male Bristleheads from females?

14. Name the only Bornean endemic which is classified as Endangered by BirdLife International?

15. Which is bigger – the Dulit Frogmouth or the Large Frogmouth?

16. When was the last known record of Dulit Partridge?

17. Two endemics have the word 'hunter' in their name. What precedes that word?

18. Which German ornithologist is remembered in the scientific name of the endemic Dulit Frogmouth?

19. The Bornean montane endemic, the Fruithunter, is a member of which cosmopolitan family?

20. Apart from Everett's Thrush, which other endemic is named after Alfred Everett?

SANDGROUSE OF THE WORLD
David Lindo – OSME

Answers: page 287

1. How many sandgrouse species have bred in Britain?

2. Name one of the two British counties in which Pallas's Sandgrouse is known to have laid eggs.

3. How many species of sandgrouse are there according to the *Handbook of the Birds of the World*?

4. In which year was the OSME journal *Sandgrouse* launched?

5. Sandgrouse have especially absorbent feathers that they use to take water to their chicks. Do both male and female carry water for the chicks?

6. It was back in 1896 when a zoologist, E. G. B. Meade-Waldo, first suggested that sandgrouse carried water in their feathers for their chicks. But when was this behaviour actually confirmed?

7. Which species of sandgrouse does not have these especially absorbent feathers and so does not carry water?

8. Which has more black breast-bands, the male or female Pin-tailed Sandgrouse?

9. The call of which thirsty species is often transcribed as '*cocktail wine, cocktail wine*'?

10. How many genera are there in the family?

11. What is unusual about the feathering of the legs of sandgrouse in the genus *Pterocles*?

12. Into which American state have sandgrouse been successfully introduced?

13. In which year did hundreds of birders go to Shetland to twitch a Pallas's Sandgrouse that stayed there for several days?

14. In one species of Sandgrouse a loud whistling sound is produced in flight by the long and narrow outermost primaries. Which species?

15. How many endemics are there in the family?

16. Which species are Near Threatened?

17. Which species regularly travels over 100 miles daily to access water in the Kalahari Desert?

18. All sandgrouse have the same number of primary feathers in each wing. How many?

19. Why do sandgrouse rub their bellies on the ground while caring for their chicks?

20. Which is the smallest of the five sandgrouse species that regularly breed in the Western Palearctic?

BIRDS OF SPURN
Tim Jones – BTO

Answers: page 287

1. Which well-known professional ornithologist found last year's Kentish Plover?

2. Andy Roadhouse recently produced the epic *Birds of Spurn*. When did Andy start birding at Spurn?

3. Who did Andy Roadhouse say was his mentor when he first started birding at Spurn?

4. Which one of these has NOT been ringed at Spurn – Spotted Towhee, Dark-eyed Junco, Song Sparrow, and White-throated Sparrow?

5. What was significant about the Woodchat Shrike reported at Spurn on 20th September 2014?

6. 2017 was a bumper spring for Iberian Chiffchaffs, but what was the year of the first Spurn record?

7. What was the wader that birders were looking for on 6th September 1954 when they serendipitously found Spurn's first Buff-breasted Sandpiper?

8. Name the winner of the 2016 'Martin Garner Spurn Young Birder of The Year' competition.

9. Spurn hosted a Siberian Accentor from 13th to 19th of October 2016. On which of those days did it also host at least ten Dusky Warblers?

10. In 1983 – you know what's coming! – a Tengmalm's Owl spent most of March at Spurn. During its stay, 25 pellets were collected and examined – one contained a BTO ring that had been fitted to which species of passerine?

11. The first Spectacled Warbler for Britain was trapped at Spurn in October 1968, but later rejected after review. Why wasn't it accepted?

12. At the end of 2016, the Spurn list had increased by three additional species. What was the new total?

13. Name one key piece of evidence that led to the 1984 Black Lark finally gaining acceptance as a first for Britain, 20 years after the initial sighting.

14. For how many swift species did the British Birds Rarities Committee assess records from Spurn in 2005, and can you name them?

15. What was unusual about the 1992 Booted Warbler?

16. Which UK breeding species has been recorded only once at Spurn on 26 April 1964?

17. Name one of the two European countries from which foreign-ringed Arctic Terns have been recovered at Spurn?

18. Name two of the three new species that were added to the Spurn list in autumn 2014?

19. A Meadow Pipit ringed at Spurn in September 1974 and later recovered in Spain held the age record for that species until 2009. How old was it to the nearest year?

20. On 22nd October 2012, Spurn experienced a near-record fall of migrants, with day records for two species in particular being broken. Which were the species?

BIRDS OF ANGOLA
Michael Mills – ABC

Answers: page 287

1. Which new host species of the Dusky Indigobird was first reported in May 2011?

2. Which Angolan endemic bird shares its English name with a prestigious American award for newspaper journalism?

3. On 20th January 1988 in Cuimba, Angola, a ringed Spotted Flycatcher was caught for display in a museum. Where was the bird originally ringed?

4. Which endemic has the Portuguese name Papa-moscas-de-Angola?

5. Of the three species named after the town of Gabela, which are Endangered?

6. Name three species on the African Bird Club checklist with 'Angola' in their name.

7. Name a species of barbet that sounds as though it has recently had a shave.

8. What is the source of the Bokmakierie's name?

9. Who named Margaret's Batis?

10. The name of which sought-after Angolan species suggests it must be seen before midnight, for fear its carriage may turn back into a pumpkin?

11. The Lubango Bird Skin Collection was started by the late Dr António da Rosa Pinto, who, in 1958, began the nucleus of the collection by leading a collecting trip to which Angolan Province?

12. Which is the largest Important Bird Area in Angola recognised by BirdLife International?

13. Who compiled the *Birds of Angola* BOU checklist, published in 2000?

14. The nest of which species of hirundine was only found in Angola for the first time in 2016?

15. Name the two *endemic* species of francolin.

16. Name the two species of double-collared sunbird that occur in Angola.

17. On 18th February 2014, which species was recorded in Angola for the first time?

18. How many species of pitta have occurred in Angola?

19. Name the two species of parrot occurring in Angola that are named after famous German ornithologists.

20. Which Angolan species's English name sounds like a well-funded senior church minister?

ANSWERS

IX

GENERAL KNOWLEDGE ANSWERS

2004

2004 A MARTIN COLLINSON
(*BRITISH BIRDS*)

1. Cetti's Warbler
2. Australia, New Zealand, Ecuador, Spain, South Africa and the UK (albeit belatedly). *Since then, Argentina, Brazil, Chile, France, Norway, Peru and Uruguay have signed.*
3. Its specific name has been changed from urbica (feminine) to urbicum (neuter)
4. 1986 (July)
5. AA
6. 33 pairs. *Now thought to be 226 birds.*
7. Curlew and Slender-billed Curlew
8. Pink(ish) [with some spotting]
9. Lance-Corporal
10. Rufous-chested Sparrow
11. It got bigger (larger format)
12. Harpy Eagle
13. West Nile Virus
14. Michael Warren
15. 1907
16. 40 beats per minute
17. Red Kite
18. 4. *Now 1 only.*
19. (*Northern*) Rockhopper Penguins
20. Myanmar/Burma

2004 B PETER WILKINSON
(*BTO NEWS*)

1. Montagu's Harrier
2. Short-tailed/Steller's Albatross
3. 1964 (Jan)
4. It is believed to be an aphrodisiac
5. They were recovered on consecutive days
6. Western Double-collared Sunbird
7. He has just had a sex change, as far as his specific name is concerned – *Lagopus mutus* (masculine) to *muta* (feminine)
8. AA

9. *Bulletin for Bird Watchers*
10. The US army's 101st (Airborne) Division
11. At the tail end of its vertebral column (the last few fused vertebrae to which the tail feathers are attached)
12. For eating too many Feral Pigeons (and Tufted Duck)
13. Cetti's Warbler
14. Clostridium botulinum
15. A dove (of sorts) [Queen Victoria and Britannia are not the right sort of birds]
16. White (with black base and tip)
17. Afforestation of the montane grasslands where they breed. *Also human settlement, sugar cane cultivation, intensive livestock farming, grassland burning, invasion by non-native trees and small-scale mining.*
18. They all had breeding peregrines on them. *Now a lot more could be added.*
19. Diclofenac. *Now definitely implicated.*
20. 12th Aug

2004 C CHRIS HARBARD
(*BIRDWATCH*)

1. Baillon's Crake
2. C
3. £38.40. *Checking on line gives a bewildering range of rates from £49.99, £69.99, £68.28 per annum to £3.99 per issue.*
4. Great Spotted Woodpecker. *Great Spotted Woodpeckers have bred in Ireland since 2009, presumably naturally. It seems that the reintroduction plans never got off the ground.*
5. Habitat loss and degradation of forest. *Twenty-one species are now Globally Threatened.*
6. Their song has become louder than 93 decibels in order to compete with traffic noise, which is above the legal limit in Germany

7. Samoan Moorhen (*Gallinula pacifica*). *Not seen subsequently despite targeted search, in 2005 and 2012.*
8. William Elford Leach
9. Weeping Dove
10. 1992 (Jan)
11. 39.8°C or 103.64°F
12. *Pectoralis major* (*superficialis*)
13. Manx Shearwater *Puffinus puffinus*
14. White
15. Streaked Shearwater *Calonectris leucomelas*
16. Woodcreepers Dendrocolaptidae
17. Hunting. *Although relative unpalatability of adults means juveniles are preferred.*
18. The central pair
19. Great Bustard
20. One month (1st Sep–31st Jan in Scotland, but 1st Oct–31st Jan in England and Wales). *Although restraint was urged in 2018 due to a poor breeding season.*

2004 D DAVE NURNEY (*BIRD WATCHING*)

1. White's Thrush
2. Increased female mortality, as they forage further afield and succumb to long-lining for Tuna
3. 1986 (March)
4. Brood parasitism by Shiny Cowbirds. *Now reclassified as EN, as Shiny Cowbirds have been trapped and removed and more protected habitat has been acquired.*
5. Oriental Pratincole
6. G
7. Inexorable Rail
8. 'Too small to twitch'
9. Nobody knows. [It is a single specimen in the Liverpool Museum, bequeathed by the 13th Earl of Derby in 1851. It is apparently related to the Nicobar Pigeon (*Caloenas nicobarica*).]
10. 4 (same as mammals)
11. John Caius

12. They are all blue
13. Hercules/Heracles (Labour No. 6)
14. *Pica* (Magpie)
15. A-laying
16. Avocet
17. 1976
18. >1,125,000. *It was >1.3 million in 2013.*
19. Hatching and Fledging Enquiry
20. The second innermost primary. (The 3rd, 4th and 5th are slightly elongated)

2005

2005 A DAVID FISHER (SUNBIRD)

1. Red
2. Chough
3. An index of population trends for a suite of lowland farmland birds – one of 15 indicators of the government's Quality of Life index. (Measurable happiness?)
4. Osprey
5. Albatrosses (and other seabirds affected by long-line fishing)
6. France. *This is probably still the case, despite the taxonomic upheavals within this species.*
7. 'Ban the Bird Fair'
8. Pileated Woodpecker
9. 1914
10. 42 years
11. Sooty Tern
12. B. E. Smythies
13. Lesser Black-backed Gull (1,116)
14. Harpist Wren
15. Calayan Rail *Gallirallus calayanensis*
16. Robins
17. 7,500
18. Yellow with 14 (Grey 12 and Golden 11). *Yellow is still correct with 16 (17 if you call a White-billed Diver a Yellow-billed Loon). There are 12 Greys and 10 Goldens, plus 2 Golds.*
19. Zambia. *Also known as Zambian Barbet.*

20. *Sylvia* with 13 (*Phylloscopus* 12, *Acrocephalus* 9). *Now* Phylloscopus *with 17 (having gained Iberian Chiffchaff, Green, Two-barred Greenish, Pale-legged Leaf and Eastern Crowned, followed by Sylvia with 14 (having gained Moltoni's) and* Acrocephalus *with only 7, having lost Moustached, which was deleted, and Thick-billed, which became Iduna.*

2005 B TIM MELLING
(NATURETREK)

1. Red
2. Blue Tit
3. Cuckoo
4. All 5
5. Hogganfield Loch, Glasgow
6. Goldfinch
7. 1,185,297. *Now it has been reduced to about 130,000 (a 90% reduction, which is excellent news, if true).*
8. An aeroplane (with 8 engines, flown once only by Howard Hughes)
9. New Zealand Storm-petrel *Oceanites maorianus*
10. Critically Endangered. *Now EN.*
11. 1854
12. European Storm-petrel
13. Grey-headed Albatross. *Quite a few circumnavigate the Southern Ocean but 46 days is still the record it seems.*
14. Pampas Tinamou
15. Italians and other 'hunting tourists' assisted by tape-recorders and pump-action shotguns. *It seems that this pathetic slaughter continues.*
16. Russia (Saratov). *More recently from Spain.*
17. Lound Quarry in Nottinghamshire, operated by Tarmac
18. 9%
19. 3%
20. Banker (in Norwich)

2005 C NIGEL JONES
(ORNITHOLIDAYS)

1. Azure (although dusky below)
2. 2003
3. A Red-footed Falcon *Falco vespertinus*. *This was a Red-footed Falcon in Martha's Vineyard, Massachusetts, in August 2004. It became known as Red Sox, appropriately.*
4. Red-shouldered Vanga
5. Their white rump
6. Wood Lark
7. Mass defaecation
8. Fringillidae (at least 996 species, although they include the Emberizidae). *HBW BirdLife only have 211.*
9. A proposed wind-farm. *The last of 33 turbines was erected in 2016 and the project manager said in 2016 that there had been no known collisions with Golden Eagles.*
10. 431 pairs. *Now 508 (Nov. 2016).*
11. Allan Octavian Hume
12. The Isle of Man
13. Firecrest, Hawfinch, Lesser Redpoll, Lesser Spotted Woodpecker, Redstart, Tree Pipit, Willow Tit and Wood Warbler
14. Barrow's Silver-eye
15. Lammergeier
16. 61
17. Barnacle Goose
18. Ivory-billed Woodpecker (not Ivory-spotted Woodpecker). *The rediscovery remains disputed.*
19. Bowland [8 pairs and 28 young]. *Sadly no longer in Bowland. 3 successful nests only (in Northumberland).*
20. 1,351. *Now perhaps 2,000.*

2005 D BRIAN SMALL (LIMOSA)

1. Flesh-pink. *Brownish yellow for the rest of the year.*
2. Hummingbird sp. *Now the back of the £10 is birdless.*
3. The male
4. Nightjar
5. 10 weeks' imprisonment
6. Eurasian with 19 (European 12 and Northern 10). *The British List now has the English vernacular names and the IOC international English names. There are only 3 Northerns on the former list – all Nearctic species. There are 32 Eurasians, 17 Europeans and 9 Northerns on the international English list.*
7. 1938/1939
8. Mallard
9. Charles Lucien Bonaparte
10. 1875
11. Osprey
12. Sobbing Pigeon
13. A drove
14. Hen Harriers. *Not to be confused with Operation Artemis concerned with peace-keeping in the Democratic Republic of the Congo, or anti-poaching in Wiltshire, or narcotic and weapon smuggling in the Arabian Gulf, or child abuse in Gwent.*
15. The nests are in a cave on mounds of guano and not in burrows
16. 1,122. *The figure has been revised to 1,125, but was superseded in 2008 with 1,843.*
17. 366 – in 1989 (There were 365 in 1987)
18. The mid-shaft barbs are weakly attached and fall off naturally aided by wear and tear. [NB. They are not plucked out by the bird itself as originally stated by Charles Waterton and Alfred Newton and for long held to be true]
19. Henna-hooded Foliage-gleaner and Rufous-necked Foliage-gleaner
20. 57

2006

2006 A ADRIAN THOMAS (WILDSOUNDS)

1. Large Mice that eat them alive
2. *Hirundo daurica* (Red-rumped Swallow)
3. Owl ('Owlet's wing')
4. Norway
5. Campbell (Island) Teal
6. *Calidris* with 17 (*Charadrius* and *Tringa* both have 9 each). *Still Calidris with 21 now, having acquired Broad-billed, Buff-breasted and Stilt Sandpipers and Ruff due to taxonomic revision. Tringa now have 10 as Grey-tailed Tattler has been tringified. Charadrius remains on 9.*
7. Black Rats on Fatuhiva
8. It was shot with an air-rifle (and the Dutch television company is being prosecuted). *The hunter from Duke Faunabeheer was fined 200 euros and the sparrow was stuffed and displayed in the Rotterdam Natural History Museum.*
9. Sparrow
10. Ross's Gull
11. Soldierbirds
12. Heron in Italian
13. Rooks
14. Ships
15. Sun Parakeet *Aratinga solstitialis. Now Aratinga maculata.*
16. 3 [Californian Condor (0 in 1987), Mauritius Kestrel (4 in 1974) and Chatham Island Black Robin (5 in 1980). (Whooping Crane was down to 14 in 1938).]
17. Cockatiel
18. Wind farms
19. 44. *It is now 50.*
20. They all may be

2006 B COLIN BRADSHAW (CARL ZEISS)

1. David Lack
2. Peregrine [They quite commonly nest in trees elsewhere]

3. Oystercatcher
4. Emperor Penguin
5. Howard Saunders [not Sooty though]
6. *Anas* with 11 (*Aythya* 8, *Anser* 6). *Now* Aythya *with 8 still. Anas has been pruned to just 5 with taxonomic reassignment and* Anser *with 7 has gained Tundra Bean Goose.*
7. Garganey
8. Hilaire Belloc
9. Endangered. *Now CR.*
10. They are hidden in hollow artificial eggs to extract blood for analysis from incubating birds.
11. Pope's Lovebird
12. A parrot (also a conceited empty-headed fop)
13. Edwards's and Silver Pheasant
14. 3 pairs
15. The discovery of gold and subsequent 100-fold increase in human population
16. Rodriguez Solitaire
17. 35. *Now 113, excluding the hyphenated bee-eater, honey-buzzard etc. The original question was asked in the era of Eurasians etc.*
18. 1,492. *1,769 breeding pairs is the 2014 total.*
19. Song Thrush
20. 97

2006 C CHRIS GALVIN (SWAROVSKI)

1. Bird flu
2. Quetzal (*Pharomachrus*)
3. A wind farm
4. Albatrosses. *Now the current score is CR 3; EN 6; VU 6; NT 6 and LC 1.*
5. Norwegian Blue
6. China (extinct in Japan now). *Although there is now a reintroduction programme in Japan.*
7. Cape May Warbler
8. *Synthliboramphus antiquus*
9. *Synthliboramphus*
10. Compressed bill
11. Excessive exploitation for their red feathers by the islanders
12. Chaffinch
13. Comice
14. Bullbirds
15. Short-tailed Albatross
16. Derek Moore
17. Pallas's Gull, Sandgrouse, Grasshopper Warbler, Leaf Warbler and Bunting
18. Albatrosses (and petrels)
19. 4,482,649
20. 32

2006 D STEPHEN MOSS (LEICA)

1. The Finch's Arms. *The Cuckoo and The Kingfisher have closed since 2006, sadly.*
2. Lundy
3. AOU (American Ornithologists' Union)
4. 5½ months (on 12th Oct 2003 at Sandgarth, Shetland)
5. Because it is named after both Jules and Edouard Verreaux (Other birds named Verreaux are only named after Jules). *It seems the apostrophe has been moved back. It was probably named after Jules Verreaux only, or so Lesson's original description would suggest. If it were named after both brothers, it would be called* Aquila verreauxiorum. *Early taxonomists didn't worry too much about grammar though, or spelling for that matter. See* ABC Bulletin, *Vol. 13 No. 2, Aug 2006, R. J. Dowsett.*
6. Crested Tit *Parus cristatus*
7. Bees, which compete for nest-holes.
8. Osprey
9. Rutland Water
10. They have all become more severely threatened and changed category for the worse since 2000 ['O'u CR→CR(PE); Nukupu'u CR→CR(PE); Maui 'Alauahio

VU→EN; O'ahu 'Alauahio CR→CR(PE); 'Akohekohe VU→CR]. *Now all are still CR except Maui Alauahio which is EN. It should be noted that there are 3 species of Nukupu'u – Kauai, Maui and Oahu – the Oahu Nukupu'u is Extinct and the others are Possibly Extinct.*

11. Monkbirds

12. St Emilion

13. Due to a bureaucratic error (nesting trees on maps were not checked). *They are no longer considered to be VU and are now LC.*

14. 1. Chatham Petrel (all the others have been introduced on to other islands to prevent all eggs being in one basket). *Now None. 190 chicks were translocated to Pitt Island and Chatham Island with successful subsequent breeding.*

15. It occurs on and near Bananal Island in Brazil

16. South Australia

17. Black-breasted Pitta

18. 1) Kiwis, 2) some New World Vultures or 3) some petrels

19. Darwin's Rhea

20. Size (The larger morph is on average 30–35% heavier than the smaller morph). *They are now considered to be 2 separate subspecies Pagodroma nivea nivea and P. n. major, Lesser and Greater Snow Petrel.*

2007

2007 A CARL DOWNING (NBC)

1. 189. *Now the score is 222, which includes 20 Possibly Extinct and 1 Extinct in the wild*

2. Skylark

3. Egg shell thickness

4. Saving Gurney's Pitta and their forest home

5. Jemima

6. 200

7. *An Illustrated Magazine Devoted Chiefly to the Birds on the British List*

8. Mrs Moreau's Sunbird

9. Cage bird trade

10. A warbler (Kiritimati Reed Warbler *Acrocephalus aequinoctialis*)

11. Magnus Magnusson

12. Old World barbets and some cuckoos. *Especially Common Hawk-cuckoo.*

13. Shelduck

14. India (more than 2,500 in Blackbuck NP, Velevadar in Gujarat; Montagu's, Pallid and European Marsh)

15. All

16. They all are, except the Great Auk (Golden Eagle in Ireland)

17. They may share the same nest burrow, but in different seasons

18. Poisoning through pesticide misuse

19. European Quail

20. 17 years. *Now 22 years 11 months.*

2007 B CHRIS HARBARD (OSME)

1. A Tawny Owl

2. Madagascar Pochard

3. Cyprus

4. 22 years

5. Blackcaps

6. Cornwall. *Very successfully.*

7. Isotope analysis of their feathers, which was the same pattern as in Senegal

8. Drongo/Dicrurus (A Philippine species)

9. Greece

10. Ruby Quail Dove

11. 1 shilling. *That is 5 p for the young, or 3 groats for the very old.*

12. Saving Northern Peru's dry forests

13. Because they providentially kept starvation at bay for the inhabitants of Norfolk Island, (although, not surprisingly, they no longer breed there)

14. Thrush

15. Hotel development. *Also plantations and a golf course proposal, mongooses and cats.*

16. Lundy and Scilly
17. A Honeyeater (Meliphagidae)
18. Carotenoids. (canthaxanthin principally)
19. The Azores (Azores Bullfinch). *Confined to São Miguel, VU.*
20. Cumbria or Northumberland – both have had rookeries containing 557 nests in the last 30 years

---

2007 C PAUL FRENCH (OBC)

1. Sociable Lapwing. *BirdLife says the population may be as high as 16,000 birds now.*
2. Excretion of salt
3. Djibouti Francolin, Bengal Florican, Restinga Antwren and Belding's Yellowthroat
4. 2006. *Now 10 pairs.*
5. UK
6. Vegetables
7. All except Parrot's Disease, which is an epiphyseal chondritis caused by syphilis
8. Rufous Hummingbird (Anna's wanders up there occasionally)
9. Bozo
10. Wind farms. *This is no longer considered a threat by BirdLife and habitat loss, cats and mongooses are the main threat.*
11. The Pelican
12. Threatened wetlands of Madagascar
13. They all have
14. At least 28 years (It was ringed in Maputo in Nov 1976 and found Jan 2005)
15. Oriental White-backed Vulture (Due to their youth, the captive birds were not expected to start breeding for at least another year)
16. Beck's Petrel
17. St Cuthbert
18. 1st February
19. Tapaculo. Pteroptochos castaneus *and tarnii.*
20. An Owl ('The Fat Owl of the Remove')

2007 D MARK ANDREWS (ABC)

1. Thrush Nightingale
2. Black Redstart
3. *The Sound Approach to Birding: A Guide to Understanding Bird Sound* (by Mark Constantine and the Sound Approach). Farming and Birds, *by Ian Newton, 2017.*
4. Ethiopia
5. Marsh Warbler
6. Saving Sumatra's last lowland rainforests
7. Papua New Guinea
8. Avian influenza
9. White-winged Guan
10. Bobo
11. Cage bird trade. *Clearance of licuri palm is the main threat.*
12. Aquatic Warbler
13. 40 years
14. 24,000
15. Chaffinch
16. Red-tailed Hawk
17. *Parus palustris* (Marsh Tit)
18. Sunbittern. *The only 2 species in the order Eurypygiformes.*
19. 13. *There are now 39 species due to recent splits and 16–22 are Extinct (There are 16 EX; 6 CR(PE); 6 CR; 4 EN; 5 VU; 2 LC).*
20. Guy Mountfort and Peter Scott

2008

2008 A MARTIN FOWLIE (NBC)

1. Preventing Extinctions: Saving the World's Critically Endangered Species
2. No
3. Lundy
4. Restinga Antwren
5. Puffin (Tree Mallow prevents puffins accessing their burrows)
6. Rubber ducks (29,000 of which fell off a Chinese ship on 29th January 1992 and have subsequently been observed in the Atlantic and elsewhere). *Apart from Australia,*

Alaska and South America bordering the Pacific, they have also reached Newfoundland and Scotland.

7. They are used as 'watch-dogs' (on account of their vocal qualities and their ability to be tamed)

8. Indonesia (16), Philippines (12) and Hawaiian islands (12). *Indonesia has 28 CR species now, Philippines have 15 CR and Hawaii have 16 CR, of which 7 are possibly extinct CR(PE) and another is extinct in the wild EW and they also have 26 extinct species EX.*

9. Pale yellow

10. New Britain Rail

11. Diclofenac. *Still in veterinary use in Spain unbelievably.*

12. Guano (They are Peruvian Booby, Blue-footed Booby, Peruvian Pelican and Guanay Cormorant)

13. White-shouldered Ibis

14. The black loral stripe

15. Rimatara Lorikeet. *EN now.*

16. Mesites (particularly the Brown and White-breasted Mesite)

17. Charles or Floreana Mockingbird. *Uplisted to EN in 2017.*

18. Immature and non-breeding Eurasian Oystercatchers

19. Adelie Penguin (Adelie Dumont d'Urville)

20. 1980

2008 B DAVID MURDOCH (OSME)

1. Preventing Extinctions: Saving the World's Critically Endangered Species

2. Red

3. A pigeon of the genus *Gallicolumba*

4. Joseph Guillemot (a Frenchman who won in 14 minutes 55.6 seconds – the slowest ever winning time)

5. Turkey. *More recently, a flock of 6–8,000 was seen on the border between Turkmenistan and Uzbekistan in 2015.*

6. The extinction of the Passenger Pigeon, which competed for oak mast

7. Belding's Yellowthroat

8. Because it wasn't until after the bird had departed that it was identified as an Olive-tree Warbler

9. 60,000 tonnes

10. Tanimbar Starling

11. Sociable Lapwing

12. Scrambled eggs on toast with anchovies

13. Waved Albatross, Townsend's Shearwater, Golden White-eye and possibly Kittlitz's Murrelet. (34,000, 46,000, 57,000 and 13–35,000 respectively). *It seems that the Townsend's Shearwater's population is probably much lower than previously thought, but Kittlitz's Murrelet is no longer CR; in fact it is NT.*

14. Yellow

15. No (after his father, 13th Earl of Derby)

16. Common Wood Pigeon

17. Northwest India and Pakistan

18. Archibald Thorburn

19. Electrocution from power lines (115 [52%] electrocuted; compared with 74 [33%] poisoned)

20. Arabian Warbler

2008 C PAUL STANCLIFFE (BTO)

1. Preventing Extinctions: Saving the World's Critically Endangered Species

2. The tail

3. Common Starling

4. No

5. Greenland

6. Arctic Warbler

7. Sharp-billed Ground Finch. *The subspecies that behaves in this way is now known as Vampire Finch.*

8. Defaecation by a bird on its legs for temperature control by evaporation (used by storks, cormorants, boobies, New World vultures et al)

9. Djibouti Francolin

10. Ruby-necklaced Emerald
11. She laid another clutch
12. Azores Bullfinch or Priolo
13. Dick Quax
14. A spear of a type used in Central Africa was embedded in its neck
15. Dark brown
16. Colombia (with 4). *Still Colombia, but with 5 (Black-bearded Helmetcrest, Gorgeted Puffleg, Turquoise-throated Puffleg [PE], Glittering Starfrontlet and Sapphire-bellied Hummingbird. [the Colorful Puffleg has been reclassified as EN]).*
17. James Fisher
18. It was accidentally electrocuted. *Sadly, other Philippine Eagles released subsequently have been shot – one shot in 2015 was treated and released, but shot again and killed.*
19. Red Crossbill
20. 1877

2008 D PETE LEONARD (ABC)

1. 190 *now 222*
2. An anchor
3. Eskimo Curlew
4. No
5. The nominate race – *Falco peregrinus peregrinus*
6. 'Willow-wrens' (Chiffchaff, Willow Warbler and Wood Warbler). *It will be 250 years ago yesterday, if you are reading this during the 2018 Bird Brain of Britain.*
7. Bluebirds
8. Bengal Florican
9. Northern Bald Ibis
10. Griffon Vulture (227 were killed). *This is likely to be an underestimate.*
11. Nightingale Bunting
12. Spoon-billed Sandpiper. *Yellow-breasted Bunting.*
13. *Pterodroma, Gallicolumba, Otus* and *Zosterops* (Gadfly Petrels, Bleeding-hearts, Scops Owls, White-eyes). *Zosterops is now the only one of these 4 with 4 CR*

species. *Now* Pomarea *(Monarchs)* and Acrocephalus *(Reed Warblers) also have 4 CR species and* Gyps *(Vultures) have 5.* Pterodroma *is 3 since Chatham Petrel is EN now, and* Gallicolumba *is 3 since Polynesian Ground-dove changed to Alopecoenas genus.* Otus *is now only 2 as 3 of the previous 4 are now EN and Annobon Scops-owl is a new CR.*

14. Spoon-billed Sandpiper
15. Germany
16. *Parus caeruleus* (Blue Tit)
17. Dark brown
18. A male which does not develop the ornamental plumage of the breeding male in the breeding season
19. 1941
20. A tornado

2009

2009 A JEZ BIRD (OBC)

1. Acorns
2. Fish
3. Amphibians (amphibians 455 species; birds 191 species). *Now amphibians 545; birds 222.*
4. Hunting licences
5. Jackdaws (a flock of noisy Jackdaws invaded the House of Commons)
6. Sword-billed Hummingbird
7. Peter Scott
8. Bob Scott
9. An adult bird taken from the wild for falconry
10. Secateurbill
11. Keratin
12. Jacanas
13. Red Kite
14. Chough
15. 3
16. Corn Bunting, Reed Bunting and Yellowhammer
17. Graham Wynne. *Mike Clarke.*
18. 1978
19. Little Ringed Plover. *588 pairs in 2015.*
20. Hungary

2009 B MARTIN FOWLIE (NBC)

1. Sap
2. Nectar and insects
3. Dr Marco Lambertini. *Patricia Zurita.*
4. Coursers
5. Georg Wilhelm Steller
6. Common Swift
7. Yes (but some do not, e.g. pigeons) [accept Yes or No]
8. Bald Bulbul
9. The puréed pulp of a bird after a bird-strike with an aeroplane
10. Californian Condor, Eskimo Curlew, Kittlitz's Murrelet, Ivory-billed Woodpecker and Bachman's Warbler. *Kittlitz's Murrelet is no longer CR, but NT.*
11. Californian Condor, Eskimo Curlew, Kittlitz's Murrelet, Ivory-billed Woodpecker and Bachman's Warbler. *(Kittlitz's Murrelet is no longer CR, but NT.*
12. 3 (Bernard, James and Anne)
13. Bernard – Goose; James – Gull; Anne – Turaco
14. The BTO
15. It is asleep
16. Jackdaw
17. Alfred, Lord Tennyson
18. 25
19. 1973
20. Angola or Zambia

2009 C RICHARD PRIOR (OSME)

1. Snails
2. Insects and other invertebrates; (also small birds, rodents, bats and lizards)
3. Charles Darwin
4. Little Sparrow
5. It ferments the leaves in its crop, whereas other birds use their gizzard to crush the leaves.
6. Cattle Egret
7. 2
8. Albatrosses and petrels
9. Spearbill
10. Sooty Shearwater (Steelhead Salmon do not cross the equator)

11. Black-winged Stilt
12. It was declared Indonesia's 'National Rare or Precious Animal' in 1993
13. 3
14. Goldfinch, Greenfinch and Linnet
15. David Snow (*Myrmotherula snowi*)
16. Sandpipers
17. Dr Alistair Dawson. *Keith Hamer.*
18. 1992
19. Northern Bald Ibis
20. Raso Lark

2009 D NIGEL REDMAN (ABC)

1. Bees
2. Crustaceans, especially krill; (but also some fish and cephalopods)
3. Henslow's Sparrow (after Rev John Henslow)
4. 1 (the columella)
5. Cuckoo
6. Brazilian Merganser, Pink-headed Duck and Crested Shelduck
7. Brazilian Merganser, Pink-headed Duck and Crested Shelduck
8. They were both killed by elepHampshire that they had wounded
9. Eric Simms
10. Weewee
11. Rock Dove
12. The Jay's blue and black primary coverts are used for these trout flies
13. It is constipated
14. Whydahs
15. Aristotle (Shag *Phalacrocorax aristotelis*)
16. Dr Andy Clements
17. Common Whitethroat
18. 1994
19. Whooping Crane
20. 5

2010

2010 A PETE MORRIS (ABC)

1. Rhode island
2. 1960s (1966)
3. 1971 (2nd Feb)
4. Iran

5. Devon. *Tufted Puffin in Kent in 2009 is a third Pacific auk, which had not been accepted onto the British List in 2010. Although this was not a Devon bird, there is a captive population in Torquay.*
6. St Kilda
7. Women's hair
8. Minute Piculet
9. Whooper
10. Mute Swan (its head was missing)
11. Mallard
12. Rimu (and also Pink Pine)
13. Blue Tit probably, but possibly Marsh Tit, but NOT Willow Tit, which had not been separated then
14. *Bulletin of the ABC*
15. Chaffinch (in Germany)
16. Drongos
17. The nutritional state of a bird during periods of feather growth (it measures the width of daily growth bars on a feather – wide bar = well-nourished bird)
18. James Ferguson-Lees and the Duke of Edinburgh
19. Myanmar/Burma
20. Blackcap

2010 B JAMES EATON (OBC)

1. Shetland
2. American Robin
3. South Carolina
4. Alexander von Nordmann
5. Lapwing (in France)
6. Skylark
7. Common Pipistrelle Bats
8. Strawberry-spectacled Tanager
9. In Rutland (north of Lagoon IV)
10. He showed that it is the young cuckoo that evicts the host's eggs and not the adult cuckoo
11. Two little ducks
12. Dr J. T. R . Sharrock
13. 19th April 1987
14. Sudan (near Sanganeb lighthouse)
15. Nuthatch
16. Cotinga
17. Doğa Derneği
18. Crested Ibis (*aka Asian, Japanese, Oriental, Imperial Crested Ibis*).

19. Canute aka Cnut (Knot)
20. It secretes a neurotoxin acquired by eating toxic beetles

---

2010 C STUART ELSOM (NBC)

1. Hebrides
2. Edward Grey
3. The 2004 tsunami
4. Thomas Gray ('An Elegy Written in a Country Churchyard']
5. 36,000,000
6. 11.3 tonnes
7. Stephen Moss and Nigel Collar
8. Utah
9. Poached eggs
10. He was the first airman to be killed by a bird-strike (A gull became entangled in the controls over Long Beach, California)
11. Samoa
12. Painted Tanager
13. Crushing birds (They are limestone slabs weighing 3–10 kg that fall and crush birds that come for the juniper berry bait)
14. 32
15. Rheas
16. Bar-tailed Godwit
17. Sandgrouse
18. Zapata Rail
19. Cyprus
20. Michael Warren

2010 D NICK MORAN (OSME)

1. Winifred Cavendish-Bentinck, Duchess of Portland, and Kate Humble (1891–1954 and 2009–?). *Now 3 women, with Miranda Krestovnikoff following Kate Humble in 2013.*
2. 2007–2011
3. Lapwing (at Aberdeen University)
4. Fair Isle
5. Dalmatian Pelican
6. Switzerland (in 1997)
7. Bermuda Petrel (Cahow)
8. Meloxicam
9. Mysterious Greenbul
10. Emperor Penguin
11. In the sky (they are all constellations in the southern sky)

12. Great Auk
13. They do not build bowers
14. Mrs Peacock
15. Haribon Foundation
16. Gerard Manley Hopkins
17. New Mexico
18. They are killed because their brains are thought by practitioners of 'muti' to assist the desired gambling outcomes
19. Robins
20. The now Vulnerable Stitchbird or Hihi

2011

2011 A STEVE ROOKE (ABC)

1. St Helena
2. Falkland Islands. *Now happily downlisted to LC.*
3. Sacred Ibis
4. Owls (Owls have now become a status symbol)
5. Twelfth
6. The Dyers' Company and the Vintners' Company
7. The Dyers' Company and the Vintners' Company
8. International Council for Bird Preservation (now BirdLife International)
9. 16 pints, 9 litres; 2 gallons; about 160 hens' eggs
10. Northern Rockhopper Penguin
11. Kate's Warbler
12. Manx Shearwater, Northern Gannet and Great Skua
13. Manx Shearwater, Northern Gannet and Great Skua
14. Kittiwake
15. Woodlark
16. Prions
17. Nightingale (to Guinea-Bissau and back)
18. Po'ouli (on Maui)
19. The Ramsar Convention
20. Aldabra Drongo. *The Aldabra Fody has been split from Red-headed Fody, so the drongo is not now the only endemic.*

2011 B CHRIS BALCHIN (NBC)

1. Pitcairn Island
2. Montserrat
3. Yes
4. Snowy Egret and Great Egret mainly, although no wading bird was safe. (He was murdered by Walter Smith, who pleaded self-defence and was jailed for 5 months)
5. Seabirds (The Protection of Seabirds Act 1869)
6. Alcidae/auks (Guillemot, Razorbill and Puffin)
7. Andean Condor
8. St Margaret's Church, Cley (where the 2008 bird has been depicted in stained glass)
9. £7 million (£7,300,000 or $11,542,683)
10. Oklahoma Warbler
11. Roger Riddington
12. It is the fleshy appendage that projects from the bill
13. Common Guillemot
14. Pigeons and doves (as they are fed only crop-milk for this time)
15. The Oriental Turtle Dove in Chipping Norton was instrumental in raising £3,131.78 from birders' donations for BirdLife Malta (organised by Steve Akers)
16. James Fisher and Roger Tory Peterson
17. James Fisher and Roger Tory Peterson
18. Juliet
19. Prince Ruspoli's Turaco
20. Light pollution (birds, especially young, are confused by street lighting and sports arenas). *It is CR.*

2011 C PAUL DONALD (OBC)

1. Henderson Island
2. Gough Island, Tristan da Cunha [probably now extinct on Tristan]
3. Starling
4. They nest in larch trees (at 2.3–4.5 m above ground)

5. They all perpetrated ornithological frauds
6. 2010 (On 10th Dec the BTO's less pleasing new logo was introduced)
7. Arctic Tern
8. 'Old Yellow'
9. Golden-rumped Warbler
10. 'Saving Spoony's Chinese Wetlands'
11. Aristophanes
12. No
13. William Blake
14. Forktail [accept *BirdingASIA* – a new bulletin]
15. Cambridgeshire (Linton) (earlier albatross records may have been other species)
16. Alien species [Delivering Alien Invasive Inventories for Europe]
17. Neither were knowingly observed by ornithologists in the 20th century
18. 1986
19. Least Tern
20. Collisions with power lines

2011 D OSCAR CAMPBELL (OSME)

1. Montserrat
2. Inaccessible Island, Tristan da Cunha
3. John Clare
4. Fire
5. Philippine Eagle
6. Turnstone or Oystercatcher
7. Turnstone or Oystercatcher
8. Western Garbage Patch, (also known as Great Pacific Garbage Patch or Pacific Trash Vortex)
9. 1934
10. Snipe
11. Eating your own dead or moribund young
12. Tristan Albatross and Gough Bunting. *These are the only 2 CR birds on Gough Island (so far), but no birds are safe from these mice, which will hopefully be eradicated by the Gough Island Restoration Programme Conservation Project.*
13. Tristan Albatross and Gough Bunting
14. Black-throated Yellow Warbler

15. A male sparrowhawk
16. Kittiwake
17. The Ornithological Society of Turkey
18. In the UK bases (by a factor of 5 times). *It was much reduced last year.*
19. A beneficial association of wild animals with humans [They nest close to villages where the grass is short due to heavy grazing by domestic animals, since the Saiga, which previously kept the Steppe short, are now too scarce to do the job].
20. They are both considered to be hybrids

2012

2012 A ANDY CLEMENTS (BTO)

1. None
2. Sparrow (bow and arrow)
3. Ogden Nash
4. Spoon-billed Sandpiper
5. 1968–69
6. Trumpeter Swan or Mute Swan [average male Trumpeter 11.9 kg, but exceptionally 17.2 kg; average male Mute 11.5 kg, but exceptionally 22.5 kg]
7. Pink-footed Geese
8. Jungle Francolin
9. Avocet
10. R. E. (Reg) Moreau
11. Central and East Asian mountains (Caucasus and Himalayas and its surrounding ranges)
12. Chinstrap Penguin
13. Petrel (Grey Petrel)
14. Ronald Hickling
15. One is a bird and the other is a cocktail (made from tequila, crème de menthe and lime juice)
16. Snail Kites (Snail-eating Couas are extinct)
17. 1905
18. Short-tailed or Steller's Albatross
19. Hilary Burn, Martin Elliott, Alan Harris, Peter Hayman, Laurel Tucker and Dan Zetterström
20. Griffon Vulture

2012 B MIKE BLAIR (OSME)

1. Australia
2. Crow
3. The Wildlife Trusts
4. 24%
5. 52
6. Giant Hummingbird
7. Citrine Fruit-crow
8. 87
9. John Gooders
10. 85 cms, 33 in
11. Orangequit
12. Yellow-eyed Penguin
13. Cockatoo ('I am the tailor cockatoo')
14. Martin Fowlie. *It is now* BirdLife – The Magazine, *edited by Luca Bonaccorsi.*
15. Black-winged Stilt
16. Henderson Island (rats) and Gough Island (mice)
17. £100,000
18. 12
19. Common Guillemot
20. Bittern

2012 C GRAHAM MADGE (OBC)

1. Australia
2. 1 (1938, Louisiana)
3. southern hemisphere (southern 23; northern 10; both 6)
4. Icterine (Scotland, 1992)
5. Lars Jonsson
6. Gould's Warbler
7. Emperor penguin
8. *olympicus* (*Cinclus cinclus olympicus*)
9. Canada (Nature Canada and Bird Studies Canada)
10. 22 million pairs
11. A Greater Black-backed Gull
12. Starling
13. Physiology or Medicine (in 1973)
14. Tanager
15. 1956
16. 96 km/hr
17. None (it was photographed by M. Penrose, a non-birder)
18. It was shot by a gamekeeper in Dumfries in September 1984 (It

was ringed as a Red-footed Falcon and only identified as an Amur Falcon post-mortem. It was found to have been of captive origin)
19. Robert Gillmor, David Thelwell and Donald Watson
20. Terry Mitcham

2012 D JOHN CLARK (ABC)

1. Australia
2. Spoonbills (14 Spoonbill young [wild reared]; 13 Spoon-billed Sandpipers [transported])
3. Tree Sparrow (sparrows were later reprieved and replaced by bed-bugs)
4. Kori Bustard or Great Bustard – Kori up to 19 kg; Great up to 18 kg, but exceptionally 24 kg
5. 10th Dec
6. They do not moult (or moult triennially or less, and they grow continuously producing feathers variably said to be 27 and 35 ft long)
7. South Georgia Pipit
8. Amur Falcon
9. 1979 (Lincolnshire)
10. Hamilton's Thrasher
11. Phil Hollom
12. Wolfgang Amadeus Mozart
13. Killian Mullarney and Dan Zetterström
14. Yellow chartreuse, apricot brandy, galliano and pernod
15. Fiordland Penguin .
16. 1) They inflict wounds at the base of the wing and tail feathers of the sitting birds and drink the blood; 2) They push the eggs and break them and eat the contents; 3) They eat the various secretions that accompany egg-laying. *A similar question was asked in 2008 but was only concerned with the vampire aspect of their behaviour.*
17. Aleutian Cackling Goose/ Aleutian Goose (formerly Aleutian Canada Goose) *Branta hutchinsii leucopareia*
18. £1,500

19. Rob Fray, Roger Davis, Dave Gamble, Andrew Harrop and Steve Lister
20. Dominic Mitchell

2013

2013 A JONATHAN MEYRAV (OSME)

1. Zero (extinct 1985)
2. Great White Egret
3. Great Tit
4. Swansea City
5. The Bahamas
6. Yelkouan Shearwater. *Between 810 and 3,241 were estimated to be killed each year.*
7. Joseph Haydn's
8. Nectar
9. Golden-rumped Manakin
10. Cape Verde Storm-petrel
11. Operation Seafarer
12. Phyllis Barclay-Smith
13. It increased (by 4% per year)
14. Because it is not extinct
15. *None really.* Liben Lark is now Archer's Lark, although it is named after Geoffrey Archer, a British ornithologist
16. Auckland Island Merganser
17. Buff-breasted Sandpiper
18. Lincolnshire (39)
19. 75
20. 4 (White-rumped; Indian [Long-billed]; Slender-billed; Red-headed)

2013 B ADAM RILEY (ABC)

1. Zero (extinct 1986)
2. Cook's, Parkinson's and Solander's Petrels
3. Clay-coloured Robin
4. A siege
5. Ascension Frigatebird
6. Rusty-throated Tanager
7. 1969
8. Spraying with pesticides by rice-growers, who regard them as pests
9. 1

10. Three-toed Woodpecker
11. The Rutland Belle
12. Polynesia (a Blue-and-Yellow Macaw)
13. Michigan, also Wisconsin, Ontario (Canada) and possibly Ohio
14. Amur Falcon. *Happily, this is no longer the case.*
15. Lord's Cricket Ground
16. Bird Fair in 1989 (ICBP became BirdLife in 1993)
17. Resplendent Quetzal (Quetzaltenango)
18. Mexico
19. Standard-winged Nightjar
20. Lewis Carroll

2013 C ADRIAN PITCHES (OBC)

1. Zero (extinct 1977)
2. Balearic Shearwater
3. 1920s (1921 in Southampton)
4. DDT (Dichlorodiphenyl-trichloroethane)
5. Lead (from lead shot – supposedly now banned)
6. Parrots (Psittacidae) (15). *Still parrots with 14, followed by Accipitridae (hawks and eagles) and Fringillidae (finches and Hawaiian honeycreepers) both with 13.*
7. Matt Merritt
8. Christoph Imboden; Mike Rands; Marco Lambertini *and Patricia Zurita*
9. 283. *Extensive taxonomic revision now has 408 species in the family Thraupidae.*
10. *Jynx torquilla* and *Junco hyemalis* (Wryneck and Dark-eyed Junco)
11. Cameroon
12. Brown-headed Cowbird
13. Maui/Hawaii
14. 2.8 million
15. Pallid Harrier
16. They have a pouch of skin under each wing in which the young are carried
17. Prince Maximilian of Wied

18. 2001
19. E. M. (Max) Nicholson
20. *Sylvia balearica*

2013 D ANDY MUSGROVE (BTO)

1. Zero (extinct 1875)
2. Switzerland
3. Snake-bird
4. Parrots
5. 1968–1972
6. 65
7. The blade of the wind-turbine, sadly. *This refers to a bird slain by a wind-turbine on Harrts on 26th June 2013, and also shows how up-to-date the quiz questions are.*
8. Because he was serving a life sentence in prison for murder (of which he served 33 years)
9. Stresemann's Bush Crow
10. New Zealand Storm Petrel
11. Pheasant
12. Yellow-necked Tanager
13. Chewing gum additive
14. Northern Royal Albatross and Yellow-eyed Penguin
15. Baer's Pochard. *Now CR, with a population estimated to be between 150 and 700 mature individuals, plus 200 in captivity.*
16. Cousin Island
17. 62
18. Lesser Frigatebird (it often comes to rest on mangroves before storms)
19. Pennant-winged Nightjar
20. The London Natural History Society

2014

2014 A NEIL CALBRADE (BTO)

1. Great Bustard
2. Four and twenty
3. *Bird Notes* or *Bird Notes and News*
4. The extinction of the Passenger Pigeon (Martha)
5. Men
6. Miranda Krestovnikoff
7. Miranda Krestovnikoff
8. Black-eared Siskin

9. Darwin's finches (it is a parasitic fly accidentally introduced to the Galapagos, which feeds on the chicks)
10. Robert Gillmor
11. 26
12. Black-browed and Black-footed Albatrosses. *Black-browed is now LC and Black-footed NT. So too are Light-mantled, Laysan, Buller's, Shy and White-capped all NT now.*
13. Poland
14. France
15. Bird Conservation Georgia (BCG) or Batumi Raptor Count (BRC) (to ameliorate the slaughter of birds of prey at the Batumi Bottleneck)
16. White
17. None (it was photographed by a non-birder, Ian Reynolds)
18. Lesser Flamingo (ringed in Lake Magadi in 1962)
19. Red Knot
20. Reed Bunting

2014 B NICK ACHESON (OSME)

1. Great Auk (still on the list)
2. 1964
3. Doyang Reservoir, Nagaland, India
4. Helmeted Guineafowl
5. 9
6. The clay pigeon
7. Red-cockaded Woodpecker
8. Red-necked Phalarope
9. King Whydah
10. Cahow or Bermuda Petrel
11. It is mainly insectivorous (there being little fruit available on Tuamotu)
12. John Cox
13. 2
14. The Tigerfish leap out of the water and catch the swallows in flight
15. 1 – Spain
16. Fair Isle; Portland
17. Dippers
18. Denmark
19. A fisherman's fly (containing a partridge's tail feather)

20. Tanzania (44 species). *Now 49 (technically South Africa has 52, but 15 of these are seabirds which do not breed on mainland Africa).*

2014 C CALLAN COHEN (ABC)

1. Snowy Owl (Eagle Owl not on)
2. Lundy
3. Diclofenac
4. 16
5. 0.3% (£1.5 million). *It would be nice to think that it is more now.*
6. Golden Eagle
7. Egyptian Goose
8. Nuthatch
9. Blatherer
10. October (397out of 734)
11. Hamerkop
12. Wood Pigeon (5.3 million pairs)
13. Muster or mustering
14. George (after George Washington, supposedly)
15. Ruddy Duck
16. *The Wild Geese*
17. Spain
18. Mauretania (at Aftout es Saheli)
19. Canada Geese
20. Spoon-billed Sandpiper

2014 D CHRIS GOODDIE (OBC)

1. Great Tit
2. Brazil, Peru, Colombia and Indonesia. *Ecuador now has 108 (and China and Philippines have both got 93).*
3. 5
4. Red Lorikeet
5. 22 (all)
6. Egyptian Vulture
7. Crete
8. Male Kelp Goose (Coscoroba Swan has black wingtips)
9. It is its German name
10. A Lanner Falcon overflying their breeding ledges (148 fledged young)
11. Short-tailed Albatross
12. In Bulford, Wiltshire – carved into the chalk by New Zealand soldiers awaiting repatriation after WWI
13. The National Audubon Society (in 1886; (R)SPB 1889)
14. Bill Oddie
15. The pupil is vertical (to protect the retina from tropical glare)
16. Great Spotted Woodpecker (Lesser Whitethroat not confirmed)
17. Treecreeper
18. A stand
19. Red-winged Laughing-thrush and Canary
20. White-throated Sparrow and Dark-eyed Junco (32 out of 99 and 27 out of 99 respectively)

2015

2015 A FIONA BARCLAY (BTO)

1. Madagascar
2. Marsh
3. Andy Mitchell
4. Common Frog (97% of vertebrate prey and 25% of all prey in nestling period)
5. 21 years (Limonia and Laburnum)
6. It was photographed by a camera trap (set up for Wild Cat, but not seen by any one)
7. Herring Gull by Ernie Janes (under a breaker in Norfolk)
8. Twice (1964 and 1986)
9. 2015 (22nd January [or shortly before] near Blofield in Norfolk)
10. Jerdon's Pitta
11. Blue-bearded Helmetcrest
12. Marsh Tit
13. Neotropic Cormorant
14. Fire
15. Karl Ernst von Baer
16. Corn Bunting
17. Chinstrap Penguin (2 males who are given the second egg of a heterosexual pair, which they successfully raise.) [There is no convincing evidence that they were homosexual – probably just sexually confused by captivity. It was the most challenged book

according to the American Library Association]
18. Dodo (possibly Slender-billed Curlew and Ivory-billed Woodpecker)
19. Oahu
20. Bill Oddie

2015 B TOM LEWIS (ABC)

1. New Caledonia
2. Hen Harrier (female radio-tagged in 2011 in Bowland – shot on a Yorkshire grouse moor in 2012)
3. Grey Heron
4. Great and Japanese Cormorant
5. Adelie Penguin
6. Skokholm
7. Salvadori's Courser
8. Emperor Goose
9. In its eye
10. Collared
11. Aphrodisiac
12. None
13. Her nose was pecked off
14. 40 years
15. 'Harvesting' of the chicks for food
16. Dhekelia, Cyprus. *In 2017 'only' a quarter of a million were killed.*
17. 356
18. 30
19. Noughties, 2009
20. 2014

2015 C TOM MCKINNEY (OSME)

1. Cuba
2. Peruvian Booby, Guanay Cormorant and Peruvian Pelican
3. Swallows
4. An egg bump
5. Yes (in Fuzhou in Fujian Province)
6. Alaska (they were introduced into Hawaii in 1788)
7. No (it also parasitises the Band-tailed Pigeon)
8. Tawny Owl, Peregrine, Hobby and Sparrowhawk
9. Malta
10. Cover your arse (tapa – cover; culo – arse)
11. Hartlaub's Nightjar

12. Once (1990)
13. Arctic
14. 22
15. Whooper Swan
16. £5 million
17. Common Buzzard. *The Stody Estate, his employer, initially lost a £222,000 Rural Payments Agency subsidy, which the Environment Secretary, Andrea Leadsom, subsequently reduced by 55%. The High Court has now ruled that the actions of Allen Lambert, the gamekeeper, were not directly attributable to The Stody Estate and quashed the financial sanction.*
18. Flamborough [accept Skokholm, which was reaccredited in 2014, having previously lost its accreditation]
19. 12
20. Wallace's Standardwing

2015 D STUART ELSOM (OBC)

1. Cameroon
2. Cuckoo. *The past tense should probably be used now as Chris ceased transmitting in September 2015 after 4 weeks in the desert, suggesting his demise.*
3. All 125 of them
4. 700 km
5. 35 million
6. Lincolnshire (39)
7. Nicobar Megapode
8. St Agnes and Gugh
9. Canary Islands
10. 11th October
11. *Alice's Adventures in Wonderland* by Lewis Carroll
12. To continue spring hunting of Quail and Turtle Doves
13. Red-necked
14. Lars Jonsson
15. Sabine's Gull
16. 120
17. BirdLife Cyprus to reduce the illegal killing of 2.5 million birds every year

18. Nearly 19 years (18 years 11 months and 3 days, recovered in Wales in 2013)
19. Nick Davies
20. Cryptic Treehunter

2016

2016 A STEPHEN MCAVOY (BTO)

1. Great Crested Grebe
2. 3
3. Hummingbird
4. Kittiwake
5. Emu – just (GS Kiwi 120 x 75 mm; Emu 130 x 90 mm [av])
6. Lesser White-fronted Goose
7. Wonga Pigeon
8. 2011
9. Spot-backed Antpitta
10. It was killed/euthanised as a voucher specimen for the American Museum of Natural History ('as it was probably more common than the fact that it had eluded rediscovery for over 60 years would suggest!')
11. An eagle, or possibly a lammergeier, dropped a tortoise on his bald head
12. Professor Jenny Gill. *Now Professor Keith Hamer.*
13. Male
14. Black
15. Kookaburra (Dacelo)
16. Chris Harbard
17. The Great Auk
18. Ibis
19. Audouin's Gull. *Now LC.*
20. Arctic Skua/Parasitic Jaeger

2016 B JOHN KINGHORN (ABC)

1. (Eurasian) Spoonbill
2. Yes
3. Yellow/yellow-orange
4. Suffolk
5. They all are
6. MK Dons
7. Crewe Alexandra (presumably not disturbed by any large crowds)
8. Pheasant

9. Silver-capped Tanager
10. Ibis
11. Tennessee and Cape May (N.B. Blackburnian is named after Mr and Mrs Blackburn)
12. Four
13. *The Thieving Magpie (La gazza ladra)*
14. Female
15. Because they had a dangerously high level of DDT in them
16. Alagoas Curassow (Spix's Macaw is classified as Possibly Extinct in the Wild)
17. Italian
18. Knot, Sanderling, Sandwich Tern, Common Tern, Arctic Tern, Swallow
19. Edgar Chance
20. Peregrine *(Mail, Express and Telegraph)*

2016 C ASHLEY BANWELL (OBC)

1. Sand Martin
2. Weasel
3. Finfoot (Heliornithidae)
4. 1
5. Arctic Warbler
6. 35 to 40
7. Black-vented Petrel (N.B. Black-vented Shearwater)
8. Black
9. Absence of wings. It is a large endangered Caribbean frog
10. Neither (they use hot sand for incubation)
11. Carolina Parakeet
12. Penguin Books (1935 – Pelican 1937)
13. Migration
14. Storks
15. Seychelles Warbler
16. Red-footed Falcon
17. Spix's Macaw. *Filmed in June 2016, thought probably to be of captive origin.*
18. Because of the illegal killing of a Common Kestrel over a junior school in Valletta, causing distress to the children

19. Extinct

20. Plastic pellets, (which are melted together to form plastic materials, but much of which 'escape' and pollute the oceans)

2016 D YOAV PERLMAN (OSME)

1. Gadwall

2. Dawn Balmer

3. 2

4. Sir David Attenborough (*Polioptila attenboroughi*)

5. Pigeon

6. Three-striped Sparrow

7. Reddish-brown

8. Helmeted Hornbill *Rhinoplax vigil*

9. 2,000 tonnes

10. Male

11. Yellow-rumped Honeyguide and Sunda or Malay Honeyguide

12. On glacial ice

13. 80%

14. Insects

15. Common Myna (House Crow is controlled and is only on Mahe and Praslin)

16. West Indies/Caribbean (Cuba, Hispaniola, Jamaica and Puerto Rico)

17. A pair of Peregrines nesting on St Michael and All Angels Church

18. Cormorants

19. Whooping Crane

20. Miriam Rothschild

2017

2017 A ASHLEY BANWELL (OBC)

1. They were both shot

2. Hoopoe Lark

3. Jesuit priest (and mathematician)

4. To ensure that, when they relaid, the next egg was fresh

5. Wales (258) (IoM 140; Scotland 63; England 7). *Now England 10.*

6. Stripe-crowned Wren

7. Barbara Young (Baroness Young of Old Scone)

8. Madagascar

9. Chinese Pond Heron

10. Blackcaps

11. Pfrimer's Parakeet

12. Nuthatch

13. Poisoning – usually deliberate

14. $11,000

15. 400 pairs

16. Hybridization (with Red-fronted Parakeets)

17. Red-bellied Pitta

18. The Falkland Islands (21,000 out of 48,000)

19. Corncrake

20. Bird of prey; Caracara (Striated or Forster's Caracara)

2017 B DAVID LINDO (OSME)

1. They were both shot

2. House Sparrow

3. Hampshire, Wiltshire, Berkshire, Oxfordshire, Sussex, Norfolk, Suffolk and Cambridgeshire

4. Bagobo Babbler

5. Yes (twice as many)

6. Iceland

7. Because the nest camera was deemed to be 'covert surveillance' and therefore inadmissible evidence

8. Broad-tailed Nightjar

9. Lebanon

10. Starling

11. Falkland Islands

12. Soldier

13. Robert Gillmor

14. Wolf and Darwin Islands (Galapagos) (recent split from Sharp-beaked Ground Finch)

15. 25 years

16. Golden Eagle

17. Dams (2 proposed dams will alter the river's ecosystem at the estuary)

18. Phasianidae, with 5

19. 2000

20. 18 years (and 2 days)

2017 C TIM JONES (BTO)

1. They were both shot

2. House Sparrow

3. They all do

4. 1,000 pairs (1,078 pairs)
5. Great Kiskadee (it was not a success)
6. Cuckoo (fitted with a transmitter in Beijing)
7. Crimson Robin
8. Magpie (Asir Magpie)
9. 11,121 (10,960 plus 161 recently extinct)
10. 6,649
11. Parson
12. Sunbird
13. Yes
14. Slaty-backed Gull
15. Udzungwa Forest-partridge
16. Cuba
17. Common Buzzard
18. Gough Bunting and Tristan Albatross
19. 11,000 (11,124)
20. Blue-eyed Ground-dove

2017 D MICHAEL MILLS (ABC)

1. Osprey (45)
2. House Sparrow
3. Chaco Chachalaca
4. Sacred Ibis (which predate eggs of terns and waders)
5. 6,833
6. Collared Laughingthrush (in Vietnam)
7. 1983
8. Fork-tailed Nightjar
9. Spokes Folks
10. Old Blue
11. Crombec
12. Engraver
13. Hampshire
14. The Waddensee
15. Borneo
16. Aberdeenshire (near Buchan)
17. Sir Peter Scott
18. Red
19. 1952
20. Not very/completely useless

SPECIALIST ANSWERS

2004

THE BRITISH LIST MARTIN COLLINSON (*BRITISH BIRDS*)

1. Tim Melling. *Now Dr Chris McInerny.*
2. 567. *Now 616 – Category A, 598; B, 8; and C 10.*
3. Mute Swan. *Now Brent Goose.*
4. 6 (7th in prep). *9th edition December 2017.*
5. Magnificent Frigatebird. *Reinstated in 2007 following Shropshire record in 2005.*
6. C
7. Birds that had not occurred in the wild state for 50 years
8. David Graham
9. 14. *Now 8.*
10. 9. *Now 10.*
11. Cetti's Warbler
12. Audouin's Gull. *Now Red-winged Blackbird (22nd Jan 2018); Elegant Tern (8th Jan 2018).*
13. 1 (Great Auk)
14. 16 (*and 13 subspecies*).
15. 12 (all except Black Lark, Brown Flycatcher, Masked Shrike and Snow Finch). *Now only Snow Finch is not on the List.*
16. Alan Knox. *In 2018 it is Andrew Harrop.*
17. None. *Still none.*
18. *Saxicola torquatus*. It is no longer *torquatus but rubicola.*
19. Masked Shrike [at Woodchurch, Kent]. *Now reinstated in 2006 following bird in 2004.*
20. Mourning Dove

RSPB CHRIS HARBARD (*BIRDWATCH*)

1. Winifred, Duchess of Portland
2. Egrets
3. The Wood of Cree
4. 1955
5. £25,000

6. Sep 1997
7. W. H. Hudson
8. 1898
9. Junior Bird Recorders' Club (JBRC)
10. The RSPB tie
11. 1903
12. George Waterston
13. The Croft, Didsbury, nr Manchester
14. 1999
15. Epping Forest
16. Respicite aves coeli (translates as 'Behold the birds of the air')
17. 1906
18. Pintails at Loch Leven
19. 1975
20. Richard Porter

H. G. ALEXANDER DAVE NURNEY (*BIRD WATCHING*)

1. Croydon
2. 3 (But only 2 were birdwatchers)
3. Gundry
4. Chiffchaff
5. Charts of song-periods of British birds
6. Mahatma Gandhi
7. Bootham School and King's College, Cambridge
8. History
9. 21 years
10. Sir NF Fromes
11. Olive (Graham)
12. Their Quaker upbringing
13. Kentish Plover
14. Hume's Warbler *P humei*
15. European Robin
16. Sociable Plover/Lapwing
17. Swanage
18. 1974
19. Woodchat Shrike
20. Edward Grey Institute

BARN OWLS PETER WILKINSON (*BTO NEWS*)

1. White (night) owl
2. 30–35 days
3. (Giovanni) Scopoli
4. 1769
5. Madeira

6. 7–8 KHz
7. **T. a. hibernica**
8. G. B. Blaker
9. 'M'
10. Hear – it helps focus the sound towards the ear
11. Middle
12. *T. a. punctatissima*
13. Banshee
14. P9
15. Brown
16. *T. a. guttata*
17. Left
18. 1937
19. 50–60 days
20. That Wicked People become Barn Owls when they die. *If they were virtuous, they became a Great Horned Owl.*

2005

BIRDS OF KENYA DAVID FISHER (SUNBIRD)

1. 6. *This could still be correct insofar as not everyone accepts the recent splits. However, BirdLife says 11 (others say 8).*
2. Egyptian Plover and Shoebill. *The Shoebill has gone.*
3. Grey-headed Gull and Sooty Gull
4. The eye is green in Great and red in Long-tailed
5. Spotted Sandpiper
6. Black-cheeked Waxbill and possibly Black-faced Waxbill. Estrilda charmosyna *and* E. erythronotos.
7. Hamerkop (Lesser Flamingo is sometimes also called 'Lighhtning Bird')
8. Yellow-mantled Weaver *Ploceus tricolor. Last seen in 1972.*
9. Taita Thrush and Taita Apalis. *There are now 6 CR species as White-headed, Hooded, White-backed and Ruppell's Vultures have been added to the CR List.*
10. Ground Hornbill
11. Black-billed Barbet
12. Ashy Starling
13. African Skimmer

14. 6
15. *Vidua fischeri*
16. 60. *Now 68.*
17. In a pack of Tarot cards
18. Colin Jackson *(still).*
19. Gillett's Lark
20. Colies

ACCEPTED BRITISH FIRSTS
(1983–2005) TIM MELLING
(NATURETREK)

1. Eastern Phoebe.
2. Philadelphia Vireo
3. Crag Martin
4. They forgot to ring it
5. Rame Head, Cornwall *1985*
6. Red-breasted Nuthatch and Swinhoe's Storm-petrel
7. 4,200
8. Brown-headed Cowbird (on Islay). *1988: Clive Mckay was the observer. His contact remains anonymous.*
9. Brown Shrike (on 30th September 1985)
10. He also found a shrike in Shetland in 1981 that was originally submitted as Isabelline, but was considered by the Committee to be Brown (but it was never regarded as wholly proven).
11. 14. It helped to distinguish it from the similar Zenaida Dove, which has only 12.
12. Blacktoft Sands, East Yorkshire.
13. Hudsonian Godwit and Red-necked Stint.
14. Bay-breasted Warbler
15. 1997
16. 106 days (11th Jan to 26th April) [although it may have been present since 8th Dec 1988, so 140 days is arguably correct too]
17. Ian Dickie – the bird being Lesser Short-toed Lark
18. 2 (Savannah Sparrow and Lesser Short-toed Lark)
19. Daurian Starling. *Still Category D.*
20. Red-eyed Vireo

BIRDS OF HAMPSHIRE
NIGEL JONES (ORNITHOLIDAYS)

1. 1952
2. Golden Oriole. *A Meinertzhagen record.*
3. Edwin Cohen
4. 1963
5. Great Bustard. *Since their reintroduction on Salisbury Plain, they have been recorded again in Hampshire.*
6. Firecrest
7. White's Thrush. *Heron Court, Christchurch, is now in Dorset.*
8. Wheatear
9. Dartford Warbler and Hobby
10. Madeiran Storm-petrel
11. Moustached Warbler
12. Capercaillie
13. 1957 (30th August at Gosport)
14. 1961 (at Titchfield Haven)
15. Moustached Warbler
16. Wood Warbler
17. Serin. *Then 10 between 1961 and 1991.*
18. Black Grouse
19. 1957 (2nd June)
20. Purple Sandpiper

LARGE GULLS OF THE NORTHERN HEMISPHERE
BRIAN SMALL (LIMOSA)

1. 5. *3rd edition, although HBW BirdLife have no subspecies.*
2. Great Black-headed (Pallas's) Gull
3. Iceland
4. 2.9
5. 2003 (October), published in *Ibis* in 2004
6. They do not. *They do now – found breeding occasionally in Galicia since 2005.*
7. The hybrid between Glaucous Gull and Herring or American Herring Gull
8. Only the one. It is a monotypic species
9. Breydon Water, Norfolk, 4th Nov 1886, shot by Johnny Thomas
10. *Larus argentatus omissus*

11. DDT
12. The Iberian Peninsula and North Africa
13. German
14. Their specific scientific names (*cachinnans* and *ridibundus*) both mean 'laughing'
15. 1997 in Dorset (1995 bred unsuccessfully)
16. Greater Black-backed Gull
17. 1811
18. Lesser Black-backed Gull
19. Niko Tinbergen
20. In the Camargue in France to protect nesting Greater Flamingoes

---

2006

THE HISTORY OF BIRDWATCHING IN BRITAIN
STEPHEN MOSS (LEICA)

1. W. H. Hudson, (whose portrait used to hang in the library of the RSPB offices in London and now hangs in the meeting room at the Lodge.)
2. Edward Grey (*The Charm of Birds*, 1927)
3. 1938
4. 'Twitching'
5. Farne Island's Lesser Crested Tern
6. Bernard Tucker
7. Bobby Tulloch
8. Pintail (Loch Leven 1901)
9. 1st June 1907
10. Jack Tart
11. 1991
12. 18 (although there were 24 for the 9 volumes)
13. Kenneth Clarke
14. Ralph Beilby. (Bewick himself wrote the text for Volume II, *Water Birds*)
15. The Hastings Rarities
16. 16 (and 13 subspecies)
17. 1904
18. W.B.
19. The Association of County Recorders and Editors
20. St Cuthbert

ENDEMIC BIRDS OF ETHIOPIA
CHRIS GALVIN (SWAROVSKI)

1. Abyssinian Blue-winged Goose
2. 14
3. 1892
4. 'An encounter with an elephant he had wounded'
5. Prince of Cerveteri
6. Its black head (*melanocephalus*)
7. White-winged Cliffchat
8. Nechisar Nightjar
9. Left
10. Wattled Ibis and White-collared Pigeon
11. Rüppell's Black Chat
12. Dr Edgardo Moltoni
13. Because it was first found near Mega in southern Ethiopia (*Hirundo megaensis*)
14. Hybridisation with White-cheeked Turaco
15. In a native hut. (Jordan Holtam reported in the journal *Scopus* that the first nest he found was attached to the roof-pole in a Borana hut and 2 metres above the floor)
16. Yellow-faced Parrot, now Yellow-fronted Parrot. (Black-winged Lovebird found at the same time had been described in 1814)
17. Harwood's Francolin
18. He was killed in Salzburg in one of the first fatal motorcar accidents. *Erlanger's Lark is now regarded as a subspecies of Blanford's Lark.*
19. J. Rouget (Rouget's Rail *Rougetius rougetii*)
20. Thick-billed Raven

BRITISH BIRDS RARITIES COMMITTEE AND BRITISH RARITIES IN THE 1990S
COLIN BRADSHAW (CARL ZEISS)

1. Seaforth, Merseyside – Song Sparrow in 1994 and White-crowned Sparrow in 1995
2. Lancashire (Pilling Lane End and Martin Mere)
3. Black Stork

4. 1995 (7th July)
5. Naumann's Thrush
6. Lesser Sand Plover
7. Red-footed Falcon
8. Nottinghamshire – Redhead and Cedar Waxwing *(2nd record)*
9. Rutland Water
10. Bay-breasted Warbler (in 1995)
11. Bridled Tern
12. Pallid Swift
13. Mourning Dove. *The 1989 record from Calf of Man is not allowable as the Manx List is separate from the British List.*
14. Spectacled Warbler
15. The Longman Outflow, Inverness
16. First year male
17. Tennessee Warbler – twice on Fair Isle in 1975, on Orkney in 1982 and St. Kilda in 1995
18. Drift Reservoir, Cornwall
19. Oriental Pratincole
20. 1990

BIRDS OF BRITAIN
ADRIAN THOMAS (WILDSOUNDS)

1. Any 2 of Canada Goose; Egyptian Goose, Nightjar and Vulture; American Wigeon, Black Duck, Bittern,Kestrel, Coot, Golden Plover, Robin and Redstart; Iceland Gull; Scottish Crossbill; Spanish Sparrow. *To which must be added Chinese Pond Heron.*
2. Corncrake – at the Nene Washes with some success
3. 1916
4. Black-winged Stilt at Titchwell
5. Rufous-tailed Robin. *In March 2018 – Red-winged Blackbird (22nd Jan 2018); Elegant Tern (8th Jan 2018).*
6. Lord Lilford in 1889
7. Charles Waterton in 1843
8. Long-tailed Duck
9. Mute Swan. *Brent Goose now.*
10. 1955
11. Scarlet Grosbeak (also Scarlet Rosefinch)
12. Wren. *Currently, it is 29, following separation from Troglodytes pacificus and T. hyemalis.*

13. Pallas's Sandgrouse
14. Rock Sparrow. *Richard Millington and Steve Gantlett.*
15. Scottish Crossbill. *There are now no Data Deficient species and 10 Near Threatened.*
16. Skylark
17. Chiffchaff collybita
18. George Montagu
19. 6. *Although only 1 remaining in genus* Parus.
20. Goldfinch

2007

ALBATROSSES CHRIS HARBARD (OSME)

1. 19. *It is now 15 (CR 3; EN 6; VU 6; plus NT 6; LC 1).*
2. Robert Cushman Murphy (in *A Logbook for Grace*)
3. The pale iris (Black-browed has a dark iris)
4. 18 kilometres per hour (11 miles per hour)
5. Western Chain in the Snares Islands (in 1995)
6. Critically Endangered. *Still CR.*
7. Light-mantled Sooty Albatross
8. Short-tailed Albatross
9. 8,000 (6,000 in Japanese/Taiwanese fleets, 2,000 in USA-based fleets). *It is thought to be less than this now as USA-based fleets are using mitigation measures, although it is not known whether the Japanese fleets are.*
10. Coastal Albatross
11. Peru (and Chile)
12. With a cross-bow. ('God save thee, ancient Mariner!/From fiends that plague thee thus!/Why look'st thou so?'/With my cross-bow/I shot the Albatross.)
13. Bermuda. (There is fossil evidence – 400,000 years ago)
14. 80 mature individuals, of which 18–25 pairs breed annually (There are another 50 immature individuals). *Now there are thought to be 170 individuals*

(100 adults) and about 26
(24–31) pairs breeding per year.

15. Japan (Bonin Islands), and Mexico
(Guadalupe Island)
16. Bristle-thighed Curlew
17. Beauchêne, Steeple Jason and
Grand Jason
18. Albatrosses are unable to digest or
regurgitate cigarette lighters picked
up as flotsam. Significant numbers
are found dead on the breeding
grounds with large amounts of
plastic, including lighters, in their
stomachs.
19. Atlantic/Western Yellow-nosed and
Sooty
20. 7. 6 *(Northern and Southern
Royal, Wandering, Antipodean
Amsterdam and Tristan
Albatrosses; note that Gibson's is
now a subspecies of Antipodean at
the moment).*

BIRDS OF CAMEROON
MARK ANDREWS (ABC)

1. 2
2. Mount Cameroon Francolin and
Mount Cameroon Speirops
3. Melba Finch
4. Nigeria
5. 2nd April
6. Bates's Weaver *(EN)* and
Bannerman's Weaver *(VU)*
7. 12
8. *boydi (Dryoscopus angolensis
boydi)*
9. Orange (with dark outer ring) (also
described as Red as well as Pink)
10. 2 (1–3 = 2.3)
11. Vulnerable
12. White-tailed Tropicbird
13. Richard Bowdler Sharpe (in 1908)
14. Ostrich (1.5% of female body
weight)
15. Ursula Davies, who was the niece
of the British explorer Captain
Boyd Alexander who described and
named the sunbird in 1903 from a
specimen collected on Fernando Po
(Bioko).
16. Black-crowned Crane

17. Michel Louette, author of 'The
Birds of Cameroon'.
18. Uganda and Zaire (Ruwenzori
Mts). *Zaire is now Democratic
Republic of Congo (and was in
2007) and also found in South
Sudan.*
19. *Caprimulgus tristigma*
20. Ortolan Bunting

THE ENDEMIC SPECIES AND SUBSPECIES OF TAIWAN
PAUL FRENCH (OBC)

1. Larger
2. 1862
3. Mikado Pheasant
4. Formosan Magpie or Formosan
Blue Magpie
5. Taiwan Yuhina
6. Interbreeding with Chinese
Hwamei, which is imported in
large numbers as a caged songbird
and which frequently escapes
7. *Euplocamus. Has also been placed
in* Hierophasis.
8. Grey-faced Buzzard (As part of an
awareness raising campaign about
the way hunting was endangering
the species, the Grey-faced Buzzard,
whose peak migration and hence
peak persecution occurs around
National Day on 10th October,
became known as National Day
Bird)
9. The skins were exported to Japan
(where they were supposed to bring
prosperity and good fortune)
10. Green or greenish-grey
11. Vinous-throated Parrotbill
12. It had been neatly plucked by its
collector
13. 7.
14. *Brachypteryx montana goodfellowi*
15. Mountain oak forest
16. Styan's Bulbul. (Styan's Red Panda
was named after him too)
17. Tea trader
18. Hybridisation with Chinese Bulbul
(as a result of habitat alteration and
also release of Chinese Bulbul for
religious purposes)

19. Bleeding throat, referring to the red/rufous streaking on the neck and throat
20. Swinhoe's in 1863 by Gould. (Mikado in 1906 by Ogilvie-Grant)

ENDEMIC BIRDS OF COLOMBIA CARL DOWNING (NBC)

1. Mangroves
2. Louis Agassiz Fuertes (Fuertes's or Indigo-winged Parrot *Hapalopsittaca fuertesi*)
3. 10. *Now 13.*
4. Cauca Guan
5. They are both named after members of the priesthood
6. *berlepschi* (*Anthocephala floriceps berlepschi*)
7. Santa Marta
8. Tolima Dove
9. Prince Albert, Queen Victoria's Prince Consort
10. Alexander Cortés-Diago and Luis Alfonso Ortega
11. Chocó Vireo
12. White-mantled Barbet Capito *Hypoleucus carrikeri*
13. 3 (*Capito hypoleucus hypoleucus, C. h. carrikeri* and *C. h. extinctus*)
14. *Bolborhynchus ferrugineifrons*
15. Gorgeted Wood-quail
16. 11. *Now 18.*
17. 41. *Now 48 (CR 12; CR(PE) 1; EN 21; VU 14).*
18. It isn't known. (the nest and eggs are undescribed). *Still not known.*
19. 5 (Stiles's, Santa Marta, Brown-rumped, Mattoral and Upper Magdalena Tapaculos). *Still 5.*
20. White-tailed and Dusky

2008

CRITICALLY ENDANGERED BIRDS OF THE NEOTROPICS MARTIN FOWLIE (NBC)

1. No (it is readily seen in Venezuela). *VU HBW says: 'common in south Venezuela, but it is rapidly exterminated once new roads are opened or illegal gold-mines established'.*
2. Mexico
3. Stout-billed Cinclodes. *It is still. CR*
4. Mangrove Finch. *Last seen on Fernandina in 1971.*
5. Black-breasted Puffleg. *Rediscovered in Cordillera de Toisan in 2006.*
6. Blue-winged Macaw
7. Indigo-winged Parrot, also Yellow-eared Parrot, which has also been helped by the use of nest-boxes, but not to the same extent. *Also Blue-throated Macaw.*
8. Isla Robinson Crusoe (The hummingbird is the Juan Fernandez Firecrown [accept Juan Fernandez Islands, as it also used to occur on Isla Alejandro Selkirk]}.
9. Masafuera Rayadito (on Isla Alejandro Selkirk)
10. Ridgway's Hawk
11. 4. *3 (Glaucous, Spix's and Blue-throated).*
12. Hooded Seedeater (A single male taken in 1823 near the Rio Araguaia in Brazil)
13. 5. *6 (Brazilian Merganser, Hooded Grebe, Purple-winged Ground-dove, Tristan Albatross, Eskimo Curlew and Glaucous Macaw).*
14. Tambito Nature Reserve. *It has subsequently been found in at least 4 other areas.*
15. Shiny Cowbird. *Following measures to control the cowbirds and habitat restoration, it is no longer CR but EN.*
16. Edward Lear, a British poet, nonsense writer and artist
17. Brazil (with 25 species). *There are now only 22.*
18. Blue-eyed Ground-dove (*Columbina cyanopis*)

19. Polylepis forest
20. Because dense Polylepis wood makes excellent charcoal

THE BIRDS OF THE SCILLY ISLES 1997-2007 PAUL STANCLIFFE (BTO)

1. Bob Flood
2. Yellow-browed Warbler – first recorded in 1867, but misidentified and not corrected until 1890
3. 4 (Common, Pallid, Alpine, Little)
4. They were found by the same observers (J. C. Harding and M. Scott, 1999 and 2004)
5. Brown Shrike (originally identified as Red-backed Shrike)
6. That was the day when a Lesser Kestrel was discovered on the golf course
7. 2002/03
8. Marsh Harrier
9. Goldcrest
10. 5 days (28th Feb to 4th March)
11. 1 (Short-toed Eagle)
12. Tresco
13. An aeroplane (DHC6 Twin Otter Scilly Skybus)
14. Little Bustard
15. Red-crested Pochard (previously 1985)
16. St Martin's
17. Pied Wheatear (previously 2001)
18. None
19. 5
20. Grey-cheeked Thrush

THE BIRDS OF SYRIA DAVID MURDOCH (OSME)

1. Gianluca Serra
2. Sociable Lapwing
3. Mourning Wheatear
4. Eastern Pied Wheatear
5. 1941
6. Bloudan
7. 13. *Now 17 (CR 2; EN 5; VU 10; plus NT 18).*
8. Winter
9. 25. *Now 23.*

10. Redwing (A Redwing ringed in Knutsford in 1976 is the only British-ringed Redwing to be recovered in Syria and was shot in Damascus in 1979)
11. Lesser White-fronted Goose
12. Brown Fish Owl
13. Israel Aharoni
14. 1
15. Syrian Serin
16. Semi-collared Flycatcher and Cinereous Bunting. *Semi-collared Flycatcher no longer NT, but Meadow Pipit and Redwing are.*
17. Smew
18. 1
19. Finsch's Wheatear [not Isabelline, which is named after its dingy colour]
20. Purple Gallinule/*Swamphen*

THE BIRDS OF ZAMBIA PETE LEONARD (ABC)

1. 1. *Zambian Barbet (Chaplin's Barbet), although Black-cheeked Lovebird and White-chested Tinkerbird may be.*
2. The Nyika Plateau
3. Swift (from Lancashire), Swallow (from Suffolk)
4. 12. *Now 19 (3 CR; 4 EN; 12 VU; plus 16 NT).*
5. Madagascar Pond-heron. *Plus now, Grey Crowned-crane, Lappet-faced Vulture and Steppe Eagle.*
6. The Bangweulu Swamp
7. *rufilatus* and *ansorgei*
8. *rufilatus* (south and west) and *ansorgei* (north and east)
9. $50. *Now BirdWatch Zambia. It seems the sub is unchanged.*
10. Parrots
11. None of them occur in Zambia (or indeed Africa)
12. Mangrove Kingfisher (in 2004)
13. An eagle (Mrs Ellison designed the Zambian flag and put the eagle on the flag to represent the Zambian people's ability to rise above the nation's problems)

14. 761 species [accept whatever the contestant says, within reason, as he compiled the checklist]. *Now ABC says 750.*

15. Pete Leonard

16. Kafunta Lodge, Luangwa National Park

17. Chestnut

18. Pennant-winged Nightjar (*Macropteryx vexillarius*)

19. Saddle-billed Stork

20. Lt-Col Ronald A. Critchley

2009

BIRDS OF ETHIOPIA AND THE HORN OF AFRICA

NIGEL REDMAN (ABC)

1. Basra Reed Warbler

2. Socotra Cormorant

3. The Jubba and the Shabeelle

4. White-crowned Starling [accept Superb Starling, Red-billed Hornbill and Red-billed Buffalo-weaver, with which it also associates]

5. One (Archer's Lark). *Now five – four vultures and Liben Lark (now conspecific with Archer's Lark)*

6. Djibouti Francolin

7. Bonelli's Eagle and Blue-cheeked Bee-eater [Trumpeter Finch is suspected, so this is acceptable too]

8. Ferruginous Duck and Maccoa Duck. *Maccoa Duck is now VU.*

9. Guy Kirwan

10. Ruppell's Robin-chat

11. Amur Falcon

12. Salvadori's, Ankober and Yellow-throated Seedeater/Serin. *VU, VU and EN.*

13. H. F. Witherby

14. 21. *Now 33 (CR 8; EN 7; VU 18; plus NT 23).*

15. *Columba oliviae* – Somali Pigeon after Lady Olive Archer

16. Nechisar Nightjar. *The purported sighting in 2009 has not been published.*

17. Left

18. The wife of E. Lort Phillips, its describer

19. White-winged Black Tit. *Now called Dark-eyed Black Tit.*

20. 9. *Now 19 (CR 6; EN 4; VU 9; plus NT 17).*

THE BIRDS OF LEBANON

RICHARD PRIOR (OSME)

1. Egyptian Vulture. *Also Steppe Eagle and Saker Falcon plus Sociable Lapwing, which is CR.*

2. Yelkouan Shearwater

3. Palestine Sunbird

4. Ostrich. *Struthio camelus syriacus has been extinct for at least 50 years, and probably longer in Lebanon, although other subspecies now occur in ostrich farms.*

5. 1970

6. Stephana

7. Charles Lucien Jules Laurent Bonaparte (nephew of Napoleon)

8. 6. *Now 11 (CR 1; EN 3; VU 7; plus NT 15).*

9. Dalmatian Pelican and Syrian Serin. *The answer is very different now. Dalmatian Pelican is now NT; Syrian Serin is still VU. Marbled Teal, Common Pochard, European Turtle-dove and Yelkouan Shearwater are all also VU.*

10. Pallid Scops Owl *Otus brucei*

11. Long-billed Pipit

12. 1984

13. 10. *It is now 11.*

14. 1999

15. The American University of Beirut

16. Rock Partridge, Pheasant and Ring-necked Parakeet. *To which can now be added Common Myna and Ruddy Duck.*

17. 14. *Now 15.*

18. 2 from: Chouf Cedars Nature Reserve, Ehden Forest Nature Reserve, Tannourine Nature Reserve, Kfar Zabad – Anjar

19. 4

20. Red-flanked Bluetail

THREATENED BIRDS OF ASIA
JEZ BIRD (OBC)

1. Red-faced Malkoha *(VU)*. *Black-bellied and Chestnut-bellied are NT.*
2. Black Shama and Cebu Flowerpecker are both endemic to the Philippine island of Cebu *EN*
3. 1949. *Although possible recent sightings in 2004 and 2005.*
4. 8 sq km
5. Great Bustard, Great Indian Bustard, Houbara Bustard, Lesser Florican and Bengal Florican. *Great Indian and Bengal Florican both CR; Lesser Florican EN; Great and Houbara Bustards VU.*
6. Hungary
7. It is invisible (Invisible Rail)
8. They are used to make drums
9. Dark-rumped Swift
10. 1964
11. Near Vladivostok (on the Rimski-Korsakov Archipelago)
12. Rufous-throated White-eye. *Now called Madanga.*
13. Blakiston's Fish Owl *EN*
14. Robert Swinhoe
15. Moluccan and Ryukyu (Amami) Woodcock. *Moluccan EN and Amami VU.*
16. Samar, Leyte and Bohol
17. Negros and Panay [accept Guimaras, where it is presumed to be extinct]
18. Caerulean Paradise-flycatcher, Sangihe Shrike-thrush and Sangihe White-eye. *All still CR.*
19. Schneider's, Gurney's, Blue-headed, Azure-breasted, Whiskered, Graceful and Fairy. *Following the recent taxonomic convulsions, there are many more species of pitta and also more Globally Threatened species. Of the 7 in the 2009, answer Whiskered has been downlisted to NT and all the others are VU except Gurney's, which is EN. In addition Sangihe, Siau and Superb are EN and Talaud, Tabar, Biak-hooded and Black-faced are VU.*
20. 1968–1978

EXTINCT BIRDS SINCE 1600
MARTIN FOWLIE (NBC)

1. Rodrigues Solitaire
2. Martha
3. 1st September 1914
4. Cincinnati
5. Georg Wilhelm Steller
6. Wake Rail (starving Japanese soldiers ate them all)
7. Mundia. *To which it has been moved.*
8. Snails (Snail-eating Coua)
9. Mauritius Blue Pigeon
10. At the Ashmolean Museum in Oxford
11. Mascarene Starling
12. Ula-'ai-hawane. *Hawaii Palmcreeper.*
13. Liverpool Pigeon
14. Réunion Ibis
15. Slender-billed Grackle
16. It was a poor flier and was heavily hunted for food by the Aleuts and sealers
17. 1852. *Seen off Newfoundland banks: last pair killed 1844.*
18. Kangaroo (Kangaroo Island Emu)
19. 4
20. Charles Barney Cory

2010

BIRDS OF MADAGASCAR
PETE MORRIS (ABC)

1. Elephant birds *(Aepyornithidae)*
2. Coral-billed Nuthatch Vanga
3. Pale blue
4. Humblot's Heron. *August 2009 at Lake Nzerakera, Selous Game Reserve.*
5. Two (Madagascar Pochard and Madagascar Fish-eagle). *Still.*
6. Madagascar Serpent-eagle *Eutriorchis astur*
7. (Madagascar) Blue Vanga
8. Vangas. *Now known as Crossley's Vanga.*
9. Red-tailed Newtonia
10. Weevils

11. 1. *From only two nests discovered.*
12. Sharp-tailed Sandpiper. *The bird was actually sighted at Toliara on 10th November 1999 and not published until 2003.*
13. 1830s (1834) Snail-eating Coua
14. Yellow-billed Sunbird-asity
15. He tasted it (he is reputed to have tasted all his specimens)
16. Old World warblers (Sylviidae). *Things have moved on and they are now in their own family Bernieridae.*
17. 3 Mesites, Ground-rollers and Asities. *Bernieridae (tetrakas et al.) is a new family. Vangas and Cuckoo Roller occur in the Comoro Islands.*
18. Yes
19. *dilutus* – Ceyx madagascariensis *dilutus* or Sakaraha Pygmy Kingfisher
20. 9 litres; 16 pints; 2 gallons; about 160 hen's eggs

BORNEAN ENDEMICS
JAMES EATON (OBC)

1. Bornean Peacock Pheasant
2. Iridipitta
3. Hose's Broadbill *Calyptomena hosei*
4. Mountain Blackeye *Chlorocharis emiliae*
5. Whitehead's Broadbill
6. Pityriasidae
7. Males lack red on flanks
8. Bornean Ground Cuckoo
9. Bornean Swiftlet *Collocalia dodgei* (formerly race of Cave Swiftlet *C. linchi*). *HBW/BirdLife consider it still to be a subspecies of Cave Swiftlet* C. linchi.
10. It is bald
11. Bulwer's Pheasant and Bornean Ground-cuckoo
12. Bornean Falconet
13. It was found, unlaid, inside a specimen that had been shot

14. Bornean Leafbird *Chloropsis kinabaluensis*
15. Blue-banded Pitta
16. Bornean Barbet (Black-throated Barbet)
17. Black-headed Pitta
18. Labi Ridge (Brunei)
19. Pygmy White-eye (now known as Bornean Ibon). *Aka Bornean Ibon and Pygmy Heleia. Now* Heleia squamifrons *previously* Oculocincta squamifrons.
20. It means 'many spurs'

BRITISH BIRD RARITIES IN THE 1980S
STUART ELSOM (NBC)

1. None
2. Sparrowhawk
3. Eastern Bonelli's Warbler and Two-barred Greenish Warbler
4. Wood Thrush and Philadelphia Vireo
5. Arab horses
6. 1982. *Cory's Shearwater, Purple Heron, White Stork, Buff-breasted Sandpiper, Richard's Pipit, Tawny Pipit, Savi's warbler, Aquatic Warbler, Serin and Scarlet Rosefinch.*
7. Savi's Warbler (1998)
8. Tengmalm's Owl (ringed as a chick in Norway 1980)
9. 2
10. Schizochroism
11. Red-flanked Bluetail. *Fair Isle and Lincolnshire.*
12. Lark Sparrow and Oriental Pratincole. *Lark Sparrow 30th June–8th July; Oriental Pratincole 22nd June–8th July.*
13. St Catherine's Point, Isle of Wight
14. Black Lark
15. Franko (Maroevic)
16. Egyptian Nightjar
17. Black-billed and Yellow-billed Cuckoos
18. Meadow Pipit (or Little Bunting)
19. Penduline Tit
20. Yellow-browed Bunting

RARE BIRDS IN THE UNITED ARAB EMIRATES NICK MORAN (OSME)

1. Red-knobbed Coot
2. Eurasian/Common Coot
3. Eleanora's Falcon
4. Abu Dhabi, Hilton/Spinneys area (by N. J. Moran)
5. Basra Reed Warbler
6. Spotted Crake
7. Flesh-footed Shearwater, found at the Fujairah Hilton Hotel
8. White-tailed Plover/Lapwing and Pied Avocet
9. 2 – Simon Aspinall and Steve James. *This would still seem to be the case, with Tommy Pedersen next on 393.*
10. On a ship off the east coast
11. Wilson's Phalarope
12. 441
13. Leach's Petrel (found dying at old Sharjah airfield)
14. Red-flanked Bluetail
15. Bay-backed Shrike
16. Whooper Swan
17. Pallas's Fish Eagle
18. African Collared Dove. *Presumably not accepted as it is not on the list.*
19. Violet-backed (Plum-coloured) Starling
20. *kalbaensis (Halcyon chloris kalbaensis)*

2011

THE LARKS OF THE WORLD PAUL DONALD (OBC)

1. Calandra Lark
2. Navy Lark (it became extinct in 1977)
3. Larkspur
4. It is the only member of the family that occurs in South America
5. Sclater's Lark in Southern Africa
6. Raso Lark
7. Archer's and Liben. *Archer's is now considered to be conspecific with Liben.*

8. Sun
9. Benguela Long-billed Lark. *There are now only 4 species in the genus* Certhilauda, *all of which occur in South Africa. The Benguela Long-billed Lark is now a subspecies of Karoo Long-billed Lark* Certhilauda subcoronata benguelensis *and it does not occur in South Africa.*
10. Williams's Lark
11. John Williams, who it is named after, was Curator of the Coryndon Museum in Nairobi and lived in Oakham for the last 2 decades of his life
12. 42. *HBW BirdLife now only recognises 28 races of Horned Larks.*
13. Degodi Lark
14. Rudd's, Liben and Archer's. *Archer's and Liben are now one species.*
15. Tibet
16. West of Kilimanjaro, Arusha area, north of Mt Meru, northern Tanzania
17. Beesley's Lark (the only site it occurs in the world). *Now a subspecies of Spike-heeled.*
18. The lark is *annae*, a subspecies of Desert Lark and was named by Richard Meinertzhagen after his wife
19. Males (25% longer – they probe more for food than females)
20. Thekla Brehm (only daughter of the German ornithologist Christian Ludwig Brehm)

BREEDING BIRDS OF THE UNITED ARAB EMIRATES OSCAR CAMPBELL (OSME)

1. Lesser Short-toed Lark
2. Red-billed Tropicbird
3. Crab Plover
4. Abu al-Abyadh and Umm Amim [accept Marawah for Umm Amim]
5. Greater Flamingo. *They have bred 10 times since – 8 times at Al Wathba and once each at Bul Syayeef and Shahama.*

6. Hudhud (or Hodhod)
7. *aucheri* (*Lanius meridionalis aucheri*). *It seems that it is now a Great Grey Shrike subspecies* Lanius excubitor aucheri.
8. Pallid Scops Owl
9. None
10. Purple Sunbird
11. Indian sub-continent. *It became Chestnut-shouldered Petronia before becoming Chestnut-shouldered Bush-sparrow* Gymnoris xanthicollis.
12. Jazirat Na'Itah
13. Amotz Zahavi
14. Saunder's Tern, White-cheeked Tern, Socotra Cormorant
15. Barn Swallow
16. European Roller
17. Three (Little Green, Blue-cheeked and European Bee-eaters)
18. Hoopoe Lark
19. Sooty Gull [Larus hemprichii also known as Hemprich's Gull]
20. 3

BIRDING IN BRITAIN IN THE 1980S CHRIS BALCHIN (NBC)

1. (Greater) Short-toed Lark
2. Ivory Gull nearby at Chesil Beach/Portland
3. Little Whimbrel
4. Robert Spencer
5. 1984
6. The Ethelburger
7. Richard Millington and Steve Gantlett and Rock Sparrow
8. Because emergency repairs and reinforcement of the isthmus were being carried out following storms and erosion
9. Evening Grosbeak in Nethy Bridge (from 10th–25th March 1980)
10. An escaped Pallas's Rosefinch
11. Marmora's Warbler
12. Cory's Shearwater. *17,230.*
13. Big Jake Ward
14. American Coot
15. Lanceolated Warbler. *This was actually 23rd Sept 1979.*
16. £500 (exactly £529)

17. Eric Ennion
18. 122
19. Wood of Cree
20. Paddyfield Warbler

BIRDS OF KAZAKHSTAN
STEVE ROOKE (ABC)

1. Crested Lark
2. I. A. Dolgushin
3. Siberian Crane, Sociable Lapwing, Slender-billed Curlew. *4 now – add Yellow-breasted Bunting.*
4. *ilensis* (*Podoces panderi ilensis*). *HBW BirdLife treat this subspecies of* Podoces panderi *as of questionable validity, due to the effects of bleaching and plumage wear.*
5. ACBK (Association for the Conservation of Biodiversity of Kazakhstan)
6. White-headed Duck
7. Strong westerly winds (Birds generally fly at high altitude over the pass, but strong westerlies bring them down)
8. Sudan
9. The building of Kapchagay Reservoir (which destroyed much of the breeding habitat)
10. 498–513 depending on the authority. *514 seems to be the latest count.*
11. 3 (Russia, China, Mongolia)
12. An ancient hybridization between Pied and Black-eared Wheatears. *HBW BirdLife jury is still out.*
13. (*Alexander*) Eduard Friedrich Eversmann. *Aka Eduard Alexandrovich Eversmann.*
14. 121. *Now 127.*
15. Large-billed Reed-warbler
16. Yellow-breasted Tit
17. *crassirostris* (scythicus) (*Charadrius leschenaultia crassirostris/scythicus*). *The name* crassirostris *has become invalid and been replaced with* scythicus.
18. 7
19. UNESCO World Heritage Site
20. 2007

2012

BIRDS OF HAMPSHIRE
JOHN CLARK (ABC)

1. J. M. Clark & J. A. Eyre
2. 1780s (1789)
3. Damerham, New Forest, 1979
4. Bitterne, now a Southampton suburb
5. 1876
6. A cat caught it, but it was rescued and released unharmed
7. 1962
8. Tresco (Scillies)
9. 3
10. Theodore Roosevelt
11. 45
12. 1985
13. 1970
14. It was shot (in 1879)
15. Mediterranean Gull, Roseate Tern and Little Tern
16. Sedge Warbler
17. RMS *Mauretania*
18. Northern Parula, Blackpoll Warbler and White-crowned Sparrow
19. 1888 and 1908. *There was apparently also an 1863 record and the 1888 influx stayed until Jan 1889.*
20. Zuid Flevoland, Netherlands

THE STATE OF THE UK'S BIRDS ANDY CLEMMENTS (BTO)

1. Common Birds Census
2. 1999
3. Foot-and-Mouth Disease
4. The inclusion of the UK Overseas Territories
5. Ramsar Convention
6. Snow Bunting
7. Hen Harrier, through concealed persecution
8. Twite
9. Fastest bird in level flight
10. Common Buzzard
11. Ruddy Duck. *'100%' decline between 2004/05 and 2014/15. There are still a handful about.*

12. 1) Asynchrony between prey availability for nestlings and hatching dates; and 2) disturbance by walkers and dogs
13. Cetti's Warbler. *1,827 in 2017.*
14. 51. *164 in 2017.*
15. Willow Tit. *Also in the 1970–2015 and 1995–2015 periods.*
16. Common Scoter
17. Henderson Lorikeet, Henderson Fruit-Dove, Henderson Rail and Henderson Reed Warbler.
18. 11. *Therefore 17 reports before the current one.*
19. Marsh Warbler
20. Spectacled Petrel (breeding on Inaccessible Island in the Tristan da Cunha group in the South Atlantic)

BRITISH BIRDS OF PREY
GRAHAM MADGE (OBC)

1. Hobby, Hen Harrier and Honey Buzzard
2. Golden Eagle. *Usually.*
3. Colin Tubbs
4. Buzzard. *A bird found dead on 27th July 2013 in Cumbria has beaten that record, being 28 years 1 month and 11 days.*
5. Father and son (Pandion and Nisus)
6. Any harrier
7. 4 (Osprey, Montagu's Harrier, Honey-Buzzard, Hobby)
8. Osprey (they are blue-grey)
9. Africa (Leslie Brown). *Author of African Birds of Prey, 1970.*
10. SW Africa (Angola & Namibia)
11. Northumberland and Gloucestershire (28 each) *In 2015 Devon had 37 confirmed breeding pairs and Northumberland 28*
12. Any 2 from Donald Watson (*Hen Harrier*), Ian Newton (*Sparrowhawk*), Jeff Watson (*Golden Eagle*), Andrew Village (*Kestrel*), Robert Kenward (*Goshawk*), Eugene Potapov and Richard Sale (*Gyrfalcon*) and Derek Ratcliffe (*Peregrine*). *Also not yet published, Sean Walls (*Buzzards*).*

13. Brown
14. Seton Gordon
15. Honey-buzzard
16. Marsh Harrier and Hobby
17. Honey-buzzard and Osprey
18. Golden Eagle
19. Lesser Kestrel, American Kestrel, Amur Falcon, Red-footed Falcon, Eleonora's Falcon, Gyr Falcon
20. Merlin *Falco columbarius*

AFGHANISTAN BIRDS
MIKE BLAIR (OSME)

1. Eagle (any species)
2. Imperial Sandgrouse (now Black-bellied)
3. Siberian Crane, Sociable Lapwing and White-rumped Vulture
4. Ménétriés's [must specify 3 é acute accents, and apostrophe]
5. Salim Ali (*Carpodacus synoicus salimalii*). *HBW BirdLife now consider this to be Pale Rosefinch* Carpodacus stoliczkae salimalii.
6. Whitish lower back (also called Pale-backed Pigeon)
7. Ibisbill
8. Turkmenistan. *Also old records from Tajikistan.*
9. Theresa (Rachel) Clay *Pyrgilauda theresae. First cousin once-removed of Richard Meinertzhagen.*
10. Surveillance. The HERON is an unmanned aerial drone and the KESTREL is the infra-red camera system it uses.
11. Tibetan and Pin-tailed
12. Collared and Small
13. *longicaudatus* (*Dicrurus leucophaeus longicaudatus*)
14. Large-billed Reed Warbler
15. 1860s (1867)
16. *picata, capistrata* and *opistholeuca* (*Oenanthe picata picata, O. p. capistrata, O. p. opistholeuca*)
17. 7 (Greater Spotted, Tawny, Steppe, Eastern Imperial, Golden, Bonelli's and Booted) [N.B. Bonelli's and Booted are now Aquila]. *Further changes –*

Greater Spotted Eagle is now Clanga clanga *and Booted is* Hieraaetus pennatus.

18. Thomas C. Jerdon *Prunella strophiata jerdoni*
19. 12 (Greater Hoopoe-lark, Calandra, Bimaculated, Bar-tailed, Desert, Greater Short-toed, Hume's Short-toed, Lesser Short-toed, Crested, Eurasian Skylark, Oriental Skylark, Shorelark)
20. 3 from Alpine, Altai (Himalayan), Rufous-breasted, Brown, Black-throated

2013

BIRDS NEW TO BRITAIN 1980–2004 ADRIAN PITCHES (OBC)

1. Golden-winged Warbler (Kent)
2. Ancient Murrelet (Lundy)
3. Swinhoe's Storm-petrel (between 1989–94)
4. 3 (Dec 1996 – Canvasback in Kent; Jan 1989 – Double-crested Cormorant in Cleveland; Feb 1989 – Golden-winged Warbler in Kent)
5. Black Lark (Anglesey)
6. 17 (the 1981 Pacific Swift was assisted, but accepted on to the British List)
7. H. G. Alexander
8. 33 years (in 1999)
9. Short-toed Eagle. *Iberian Chiffchaff has recently usurped Short-toed Eagle by breeding in Wales.*
10. October (19)
11. Marmora's Warbler (South Yorkshire). *15th May to 22nd July*
12. Red breasted Nuthatch. *13th Oct 1989 to at least 6th May 1990.*
13. Charles Wilkins
14. 9
15. None (claims of Thayer's Gull and Elegant Tern have not yet been accepted). *Elegant Tern has recently been added.*
16. Philadelphia Vireo

17. None (although the Pacific Swift at Cley was the first to reach British airspace unaided. *As the 1981 'first' was an exhausted bird trying to land on a man's shoulder on a North Sea gas platform 45 km from shore.*

18. 6 – Magnolia, Chestnut-sided, Wilson's, Blackburnian, Golden-winged and Bay-breasted

19. Lesser Scaup (163)

20. 2. *Brown Shrike and Chestnut-sided Warbler – both in 1985.*

POPULATION ESTIMATES FOR BIRDS OF BRITAIN
ANDY MUSGROVE (BTO)

1. Knot
2. 5
3. Razorbill
4. Wryneck; Lesser Spotted Woodpecker; Green Woodpecker; Great Spotted Woodpecker
5. Wren. *8.6 million in UK.*
6. 140
7. Guillemot
8. Leach's Petrel
9. Blackbird; Song Thrush; Mistle Thrush; Ring Ouzel
10. Savi's Warbler
11. 150
12. 596 (i.e. Categories A, B and C of the British List). *It is now 616.*
13. Jackdaw
14. Little Egret. *921 is the most recent score.*
15. 15
16. Willow Warbler
17. Tawny Owl
18. Mandarin Duck
19. Wood Pigeon (5.3 million pairs)
20. 12 or 13 million

BIRDS OF SOUTH AFRICA
ADAM RILEY (ABC)

1. Blue Crane
2. Brilpikkewyn
3. Speckled, White-backed, Red-faced

4. Finfoots Heliornithidae [accept also Skimmers Rynchopidae]. *African Skimmer is a rare vagrant to South Africa but has bred historically in Zululand.*

5. Tristan Albatross. *Sadly, White-winged Flufftail and White-headed, White-backed and Hooded Vultures must be added.*

6. Chaetopidae (Rockjumpers)

7. 15

8. Taita Falcon

9. Dec 1912

10. Marabou Stork

11. Neddicky

12. 6

13. Darters. *Anhingidae.*

14. *Zosterops senegalensis* (African Yellow White-eye)

15. 41. *It is now 52 (CR 5; EN 21; VU 26; plus NT 37).*

16. Spotted Flycatcher

17. Eaton's Pintail

18. Ground Woodpecker

19. 7

20. 6 (White-backed, Hooded, Egyptian, Cape, Lappet-faced, White-headed)

DESERT BIRDS OF ISRAEL
JONATHAN MEYRAV (OSME)

1. 3
2. Sociable Lapwing; Northern Bald Ibis
3. Egyptian Vulture
4. Macqueen's has black feathers in its crest; Houbara has a purely white crest
5. 15
6. Black-bellied Sandgrouse
7. Desert Lark
8. Pale cream-brown or dingy yellowish-grey colour (possibly after Queen Isabella of Castile, who promised not to change her undergarments until Spain was freed from the Moors (in 1492). *Although also attributed to Isabel Clara Eugenia, wife of the Archduke of Austria who was*

beseiged in Ostend in 1601 by her brother Philip III with the same promise/threat.

9. Namaqua Dove
10. 3 – Bunting, Storm-petrel, Warbler
11. 4. *1 only (HBW BirdLife have separated the other 3 races to Pale Rosefinch Carpodacus stoliczkae).*
12. Thick-billed Lark *Rhamphocoris clotbey* (after Antoine Clot, known as Clot Bey)
13. Fea's Petrel [accept Soft-plumaged Petrel *(as it was originally described)*]
14. Hume's Tawny Owl *Strix butleri*
15. Saker Falcon; Egyptian Vulture. *And Lappet-faced Vulture.*
16. Least Concern
17. 6 – Northern, Isabelline, Pied, Black-eared, White-crowned Black, Desert
18. 16 days
19. Quail
20. Houbara Bustard (now considered to have been Macqueen's). *It was the same species nonetheless, i.e. Macqueen's.*

2014

THE ENDEMIC BIRDS OF MADAGASCAR CALLAN COHEN (ABC)

1. Madagascar Pochard
2. Red-shouldered Vanga (Phoebe Snetsinger died in a car accident on her trip to see it)
3. 3
4. Meller's Duck, Madagascar Teal, Madagascar Pochard
5. Madagascan Snipe
6. Sickle-billed Vanga
7. Pitta-like Ground Roller
8. Tcha-chert-be is a Malagasy name for vangas
9. Over 3 metres
10. Madagascar Pratincole
11. Long-billed Greenbul alias Common Tetraka or Madagascar

Greenbul. *This is now Long-billed Tetraka Bernieria madagascariensis. The family Bernieridae now includes 8 genera.*
12. 3
13. Blue-grey
14. Pink Pigeon from Mauritius. *They are the only 2 extant members of the genus Nesoenas.*
15. Chameleons and Leaf-tailed Geckos (snakes only form 1.5%)
16. Far Eastern Curlew *Numenius madagascariensis. It probably should have been* macassarensis *after Macassar in Sulawesi/ Celebes.*
17. The coital act is greatly prolonged for as long as 30 minutes
18. Malagasy Crowned Eagle
19. Saving Madagascar's Fragile Wetlands
20. Madagascan or Black-banded Plover and Madagascar or Humblot's Heron

---

PITTAS OF ASIA CHRIS GOODDIE (OBC)

1. Indian Pitta
2. Gurney's Pitta
3. Eared pitta (aka Phayre's Pitta *Pitta phayrei*) Phayre's Leaf Monkey
4. Blue-winged Pitta
5. Vulnerable
6. Mangrove Pitta
7. Ivory-breasted Pitta
8. Schneider's, Azure-breasted and Whiskered Pittas
9. Schneider's, Azure-breasted and Whiskered Pittas
10. Ivory-breasted Pitta
11. It was erroneously thought to have come from Guiana. *Now Javan-banded Pitta, separated from Bornean and Malay-banded Pittas, but still* Pitta guajanus.
12. Pitta patta
13. 8 (Giant, Banded, Blue-headed, Blue-banded, Garnet, Hooded [resident], Fairy and Blue-winged [northern hemisphere winter

migrants]). 9 (*Bornean, Western and Black-crowned*).

14. It comes from a local language in India – Telegu from Andhra Pradesh (the word variously means 'small bird', 'pretty bauble' or 'pet')
15. Schneider's Pitta
16. 2,980 metres. Blue-winged Pitta, found in the province of Gansu, in central China.
17. Louis Jean Pierre Vieillot in 1816
18. Indian, Fairy and Blue-winged (also some Hooded of subspecies *cucullata*)
19. Gurney's
20. Fairy Pitta

STONE-CURLEWS
NEIL CALBRADE (BTO)

1. Africa or Asia (both have 4)
2. *Burhinus indicus* Indian Stone-curlew (formerly treated as a subspecies of Eurasian Stone-curlew)
3. 5: *distinctus, insularum, saharae, oedicnemus* and *harterti* [*indicus* is a separate species now]
4. The swollen joint between the tibia and tarsus, its 'thick knee'
5. Sierra Leone and Ghana
6. Norfolk. *In 2015 Norfolk with 99 confirmed pairs just beat Suffolk with 96 and Wiltshire with 90.*
7. 22 years 4 months 1 day
8. (*Burhinus oedicnemus*) *insularum* or *distinctus*
9. Nowhere – it is a resident population
10. Lindisfarne Castle, Northumberland
11. 1957
12. Jaundice
13. Water Dikkop
14. 1758
15. Spotted Dikkop
16. Double-striped Thick-knee
17. Flat roofs of houses
18. Beach Thick-knee is exclusively coastal; Greater Thick-knee also breeds along rivers and beside lakes.
19. Triel
20. 24–27 days

THREATENED WATERFOWL
NICK ACHESON (OSME)

1. 1949. *Although there is a possible sighting in 2004 and credible local reports in 2005.*
2. Endangered
3. White-winged Duck
4. 6
5. Crested Shelduck, Laysan Duck, Pink-headed Duck, Baer's Pochard, Madagascar Pochard, Brazilian Merganser
6. *Hymenolaimus malacorhynchos*
7. Auckland Merganser
8. Head-high-tail-cock
9. Rivers
10. 1981
11. 1964
12. North Korea. *There have been further unsubstantiated reports from China up until 1990.*
13. 1991. *Strictly speaking 1992, as it was taken into captivity and died in Antananarivo Zoological and Botanical Gardens in 1992.*
14. Laysan Duck
15. Salvadori's Teal (Roy Salvadori won Le Mans in 1959)
16. Sikhote-Alin
17. Poor duckling survival caused by a very limited invertebrate food supply for ducklings. *Siltation from slash and burn etc. Reintroduction to a suitable lake of the captive population may be possible soon.*
18. Serra da Canastra National Park
19. Minas Gerais
20. 2,500–2,800 g or 88–98 oz or 5½–6¼ lbs

2015

BIRDS IN THE MUSIC OF OLIVIER MESSIAEN
TOM MCKINNEY (OSME)

1. Hoopoe
2. A lighthouse siren or foghorn
3. Jura
4. 13
5. Alpine Chough
6. Black Wheatear

7. Song Thrush
8. John Gould
9. Greater Prairie Chicken (Vulnerable)
10. *La Nativité du Seigneur*
11. *Un oiseau des arbres de vie*
12. Subalpine Warbler
13. Chinese Thrush and Canyon Wren
14. Xylophone and marimba
15. 'Indian Minah' or Common Myna (as now known)
16. Northern Mockingbird and Wood Thrush
17. *Saint François d'Assise*
18. Blackbird
19. Gerygone. *Fan-tailed Gerygone.*
20. Piccolo, glockenspiel and xylophone

RARE BIRDS IN BRITAIN IN THE 1980S STUART ELSOM (OBC)

1. Grey-cheeked Thrush
2. 2
3. Tengmalm's Owl was suppressed at Spurn Point
4. Mourning Dove (on a steel structure from Texas imported via Rotterdam)
5. 1988 and 1989
6. Meadow Pipit or Little Bunting
7. Ovenbird
8. Egyptian Nightjar on Portland Bill
9. 3. *Hermit, Grey-cheeked and Swainson's.*
10. St. Catherine's Point, Isle of Wight (on 16th May 1985)
11. Red-breasted Nuthatch
12. 1985 (if 4 is an invasion)
13. All were initially thought to have been firsts for Britain in the 1980s but were relegated to seconds after the acceptance of records from previous decades
14. 5. Magnolia, Chestnut-sided, Wilson's, Blackburnian and Golden-winged (although the first Blackburnian was seen in 1961 but added in the 1980s)
15. Skomer Island, Pembrokeshire
16. Cleveland (or Yorkshire) and Scilly

17. All 4 places had Black-billed Cuckoos there in 1982
18. Brown Shrike
19. White's Thrush with 2 records (Siberian Thrush with 1, although also 1 in Ireland)
20. Crag Martin

NOTABLE FEMALE FIGURES IN BIRDING FIONA BARCLAY (BTO)

1. None
2. Dawn Balmer
3. Dr Debbie Pain. *Now CEO of World Land Trust.*
4. The Duchess of Portland, Winifred Anna Cavendish-Bentinck (1891–1954)
5. 3. *The Duchess of Portland, Kate Humble and Miranda Krestovnikoff.*
6. Eileen Rees
7. Nancy Gull
8. Stephanie Tyler
9. Red-shouldered Vanga
10. Dr Claire Spottiswoode
11. Professor Jenny Gill
12. 1889
13. Joan Hall-Craggs and Dorothy Vincent
14. Hilary Burn
15. Theresa Clay
16. Janet Kear
17. S(tephana) Vere Benson (Mrs H. T. Hillier)
18. Angela Turner
19. Laurel Tucker
20. Barbara Young

THE ENDEMIC BIRDS OF SAO TOME TOM LEWIS (ABC)

1. São Tomé Fiscal, São Tomé Grosbeak and Dwarf Olive Ibis (if you consider this is a species). *HBW BirdLife does.*
2. Tom Gullick
3. Yellow or greenish-yellow
4. São Tomé Weaver
5. São Tomé Scops-Owl
6. Forest degradation (which is creating more suitable habitat for them)

7. Colonel Francisco (Xavier O'Kelly de Aguilar Azeredo) Newton Newton's Sunbird (*Anabathmis newtonii*) & São Tomé Fiscal (*Lanius newtoni*)
8. Giant Weaver
9. Four. *Maroon Pigeon* Columba thomensis, *São Tomé Spinetail* Zoonavena thomensis, *Sao Tome Sunbird* Dreptes thomensis, *Sao Tome Kingfisher* Corythornis thomensis
10. Harlequin Quail. Coturnix delagorguei histrionica.
11. Palm-wine
12. Bocage's Longbill
13. Hunting
14. Golden or yellow
15. Dwarf Ibis or Dwarf Olive Ibis
16. Malachite Kingfisher
17. Red or pinkish-red
18. J. P. Chapin
19. Stout beak
20. Figs

15. Grey Crowned-crane
16. 3 – Buff-spotted, Red-chested and Streaky-breasted
17. Slender-billed Flufftail of Madagascar
18. 4 (white, red, chestnut, buff)
19. Buff-spotted (7,500,000 sq km)
20. Buff-spotted – up to 60 g

SONGS AND CALLS OF EUROPEAN BIRDS
STEPHEN MCAVOY (BTO)

1. Raven
2. Cuckoo
3. 'Mixed Singers'
4. Common Eider
5. Water Rail
6. Willow Warbler, Chiffchaff and Wood Warbler
7. Bittern
8. Stone-curlew
9. Marsh Warbler
10. Cuckoo, Nightingale and Quail
11. Above
12. It is double-noted
13. Great Auk
14. Caucasian Snowcock
15. The Nightingale
16. Capercaillie
17. Skylark (*The Lark Ascending*)
18. Ludwig Koch
19. Pacific Golden Plover
20. Mute Swan

2016

FLUFFTAILS OF THE WORLD
JOHN KINGHORN (ABC)

1. None. They all do
2. Finfoots [Finfeet?](Heliornithidae). *HBW BirdLife still include them with Rallidae.*
3. Male
4. The domestic cat
5. White-spotted Flufftail (*Sarothrura pulchra*) (means 'beautiful broom tail')
6. Slender-billed Flufftail – Endangered and White-winged Flufftail – Critically Endangered)
7. Both are found in dense forest (the rest are grassland/marsh dwellers)
8. White
9. 1
10. Anjozorobe.
11. White-spotted Flufftail
12. Buff-spotted Flufftail
13. Witvlerkveikuiken
14. Streaky-breasted Flufftail (White-winged Flufftail may migrate also)

ENDEMIC BIRDS OF SUMATRA
ASHLEY BANWELL (OBC)

1. White
2. Mega Island
3. Sumatran Ground Cuckoo, Silvery Pigeon, Rück's Blue Flycatcher. *Silvery Pigeon is probably not a proper endemic as it has been recorded in Borneo. However, Nias Hill Myna has been split from Common Hill Myna and is CR.*
4. Streaked Bulbul, Striated Bulbul, Sumatran Bulbul. *There is also a Striated Bulbul* Pycnonotus striatus, *although its range does not overlap.*

5. Sumatran Cochoa
6. Walter Rothschild
7. They are identical to the human ear
8. Hair-crested Drongo
9. 2. Turdus poliocephalus loeseri *and* T. p. indrapurae
10. Rück's Blue Flycatcher
11. Rusty-breasted Wren-babbler
12. A clear piping 'hi-hi-hi-hi-hi-huuuuh' or 'ip'ip'ip'ip'ip-puuuuuh' (with c. 4–6 short notes), lasting 1·2–1·6 seconds
13. They shed feathers
14. Bright sky-blue
15. Mentawai Scops Owl, Simulue Scops Owl, Enggano Scops Owl, Engganno White eye. *And Nias Hill Myna*
16. Near Threatened
17. Short-tailed (or Sumatran) Frogmouth
18. 1936
19. Sumatran Babbler *Trichastoma buettikofer*
20. 1916. *There have been subsequent sightings.*

RARE BIRDS IN ISRAEL FROM 1985 TO THE PRESENT DAY
YOAV PERLMAN (OSME)

1. Crab Plover
2. 2010
3. Didric Cuckoo
4. 4
5. Grasshopper Warbler
6. Radde's Accentor
7. Common Goldeneye
8. It was the first documented spring record
9. Kestrel
10. Southern Pochard
11. (Yoav gets a point if he comes up with a) any respectable reason, alibi, defence, explanation or mitigation; or b) despicable abuse of the other two). As far as I can see Messrs Mizrachi and Granit are now both on 475 and Yoav is equal third still on 463 with Oz Horine.

12. It was startled by a boat.
13. A soccer field near Eilat's hotels.
14. 2012 (May)
15. 1 (in 2012)
16. 3 (in 1991, 1992 and 1998)
17. Ashy Drongo
18. Asian Desert Warbler
19. December 2009, still present in January 2010
20. Tree Sparrow

2017

ENDEMIC BIRDS OF BORNEO
ASHLEY BANWELL (OBC)

1. Bristlehead, *Pityriasis* (literally 'bran' or 'flaky skin')
2. Black-browed Babbler
3. Data Deficient
4. Black throat of Whitehead's and blue belly of Hose's
5. Whitehead's Trogon, Broadbill and Spiderhunter
6. Bornean Stubtail *Urosphena whiteheadi* Fruithunter *Chlamydochaera jefferyi*
7. 1880s (1885–88)
8. 3 (Mountain, Golden-naped, Bornean)
9. Sumatra Ground Cuckoo
10. Oculocincta to Heleia
11. Red legs and blue facial skin
12. Crimson-headed Partridge *Haematortyx sanguiniceps*
13. Males lack red on flanks
14. Bornean Peacock Pheasant. *Although this question was asked in 2010 and the answer was correct at March 2018, it is worth noting that there are 5 Vulnerable endemics – Dulit Partridge, Bulwer's Pheasant, Kinabalu Serpent-eagle, Blue-headed Pitta and Bornean Wren-babbler.*
15. Large
16. 1937 (there have been unconfirmed reports since)
17. Fruit and Spider
18. Ernst Hartert – *Batrachostomus harterti*

19. Turdidae

20. Chestnut-crested (*Yuhina Yuhina everetti*)

SANDGROUSE OF THE WORLD
DAVID LINDO (OSME)

1. 1 (Pallas's Sandgrouse bred after the 1888/89 invasion)

2. Yorkshire and Morayshire [accept Elginshire]

3. 16

4. 1980

5. No, it is just the male

6. 1960

7. Tibetan Sandgrouse

8. Female (3 black bands versus the male's 2)

9. Namaqua Sandgrouse (whose call is a characteristic 'kelkiewyn, kelkiewyn')

10. 2

11. They are feathered only at the front of the tarsometatarsi

12. Hawaii. *Chestnut-bellied. Also introduced unsuccessfully into Nevada.*

13. 1990

14. Pallas's Sandgrouse

15. 1. *Madagascar.*

16. None

17. Burchell's Sandgrouse

18. 11

19. To remove the waterproof oils so they can absorb water for their chicks

20. Lichtenstein's Sandgrouse (at 22–25 cms)

BIRDS OF SPURN
TIM JONES (BTO)

1. Andy Clements

2. August 1980

3. John Cudworth

4. Dark-eyed Junco

5. It was subsequently re-identified as Britain's third Masked Shrike

6. 2004

7. Stilt Sandpiper (Spurn's first and only)

8. George Dunbar. *Dante Shepherd is the 2017 winner*

9. 15th October

10. Tree Sparrow. *There was much muttering (and more) among the knowledgeable audience, who felt that the answer should have been Treecreeper, the answer given by the contestant. To avoid a riot he was allowed his answer. The reason for the problem was that a Treecreeper's wing had also been found in a pellet and presumably the contestant and the members of the audience had misheard the word 'ring' as 'wing'. I don't think Stephen Moss has a lisp. (Not helped by the adjudicator's presbyacusis.)*

11. Because it was later identified as a Subalpine Warbler

12. 394

13. 1) The rediscovery of original observer Nick Bell's 'lost' notebook in his mum's attic in 1996; 2) the subsequent unearthing of the original description in the Spurn Bird Observatory logbook; 3) submission of field notes by a second, independent observer, Alex Cruickshanks.

14. 4: Chimney, Pacific, Pallid, Alpine (dropped by BBRC in 2006).

15. It was a singing male that held territory between 11th–22nd June (rather than a late August–late September migrant)

16. Cirl Bunting

17. Germany and Estonia

18. Masked Shrike, Blackpoll Warbler and Steller's Eider

19. 7 years 2 months

20. Redwing (21,100) and Brambling (2,675)

BIRDS OF ANGOLA
MICHAEL MILLS (ABC)

1. Dusky Twinspot

2. Pulitzer's Longbill

3. Cashel, Tipperary, Ireland (on 23rd June 1984, ringed as a chick)
4. Angola Slaty Flycatcher
5. All 3 (Helmet-shrike, Bush-shrike and Akalat)
6. Angola Lark, Angola Swallow, Angola Cave-chat, Angola Slaty Flycatcher, Angola Batis – also Angolan Cliff Swallow
7. Naked-faced Barbet
8. It's onomatopoeic (the typical call can be rendered 'bok-bok-mak-kik')
9. Wolfrid Rudyerd Boulton (after his first wife)
10. Cinderella Waxbill
11. The Moxico Province, in the east of the country
12. Iona National Park (1,592,000 ha)
13. W. R. J. (Richard) Dean
14. Brazza's Martin
15. Grey-striped and Swierstra's Francolin
16. Miombo and Ludwig's Double-collared Sunbirds. *Aka Western Miombo and Montane.*
17. Pacific Golden Plover
18. Only 1 (African Pitta)
19. Meyer's Parrot and Rüppell's Parrot
20. Golden-backed Bishop